KV-042-761

Simple Justice

DRILL HALL LIBRARY
MEDWAY

WITHDRAWN
MEDWAY
LIBRARY

MWJITSSPSSR
10003944

3032174

Simple Justice

Charles Murray

Commentaries

Rob Allen
John Cottingham
Christie Davies
J.C. Lester
Tom Sorrell
Vivien Stern

Edited by

David Conway

Civitas: Institute for the Study of Civil Society
in association with the *Sunday Times*

London
Registered Charity No. 1085494

First published June 2005

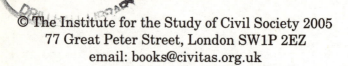

© The Institute for the Study of Civil Society 2005
77 Great Peter Street, London SW1P 2EZ
email: books@civitas.org.uk

Independence: The Institute for the Study of Civil Society (CIVITAS) is a registered educational charity (No. 1085494) and a company limited by guarantee (No. 04023541). CIVITAS is financed from a variety of private sources to avoid over-reliance on any single or small group of donors.

All publications are independently refereed. All the Institute's publications seek to further its objective of promoting the advancement of learning. The views expressed are those of the authors, not of the Institute.

All rights reserved

ISBN 1-903 386-44 6

Acknowledgement

Charles Murray's essay first appeared in two parts in the *Sunday Times* in January 2004. Civitas is grateful to its editor, John Witherow, for kind permission to reproduce the material here.

Typeset by Civitas
in New Century Schoolbook

Printed in Great Britain by
St Edmundsbury Press
Bury St Edmunds, Suffolk IP33 3TU

Contents

Authors

Charles Murray is W.H.Brady Scholar at the American Enterprise Institute for Public Policy Research based in Washington DC. His several books include *Losing Ground: American Social Policy 1950-1980*, *In Pursuit of Happiness and Good Government*, *The Bell Curve: Intelligence and Class Structure in American Life* (with Richard Hernnstein), and *Human Accomplishment: The Pursuit of Excellence in the Arts and Sciences, 800 B.C. to 1950*. He is also author of *Charles Murray and the Underclass*, *Underclass + 10* and *Does Prison Work?* published by Civitas in association with the *Sunday Times*.

Rob Allen is director of the International Centre for Prison Studies at the University of London and was previously director of Rethinking Crime and Punishment, an initiative set up by the Esmée Fairbairn Foundation to change public attitudes to prison and alternatives. Before that he was director of research and development at the crime reduction charity, NACRO. He has been a member of the Youth Justice Board for England and Wales since 1998. He has written widely on crime and punishment including 'Children and Crime: Taking Responsibility' for the IPPR. Rob has undertaken work on criminal justice reform in 14 countries.

David Conway is a Senior Research Fellow at Civitas and Emeritus Professor of Philosophy at Middlesex University. His publications include: *Classical Liberalism: The Unvanquished Ideal* and *In Defence of the Realm: The Place of Nations in Classical Liberalism*.

John Cottingham is Professor of Philosophy and Director of Research in the School of Humanities at the University of Reading, and is an Honorary Fellow of St John's College Oxford. He has published widely on Descartes and the seventeenth-century rationalists, and also on moral philosophy and philosophy of religion. His *On the Meaning of Life*

(Routledge) appeared in 2003, and his *The Spiritual Dimension: Religion, Philosophy and Human Value* is to be published by Cambridge University Press in 2005.

Christie Davies was educated at Emmanuel College Cambridge where he took a double first in Economics and a PhD in Social and Political Sciences and was both a scholar of the College and Wrenbury scholar in Political Economy. He is the co-author of *Wrongful Imprisonment*, 1973 and author of *The Strange Death of Moral Britain*, 2004. He is also the author of many articles in criminology journals and has been consulted by the Law Commission and by barristers. He has lectured on crime and the law in Britain, Greece, Hungary and the United States and has given many papers at criminology and social history conferences.

J.C. Lester has taught philosophy and political theory at various universities including the London School of Economics. His specialism is libertarianism. He has articles on libertarian issues, including crime and restitution, in many scholarly periodicals. In his *Escape From Leviathan* he develops a new theory of interpersonal liberty while offering a philosophical defence of the social scientific evidence that private-property anarchy best promotes both liberty and human welfare. He is currently writing a dictionary of anti-politics.

Tom Sorell is Professor of Philosophy at the University of Essex. He has published widely on punishment and capital punishment.

Vivien Stern CBE is Senior Research Fellow at the International Centre for Prison Studies (ICPS) at King's College, London. She is also Honorary Secretary General of Penal Reform International (PRI), a non-governmental organisation promoting penal reform throughout the world. From 1977 to 1996 Vivien Stern was Director of the National Association for the Care and Resettlement of Offenders (NACRO). In 2003 she became the Convenor of the

Scottish Consortium on Crime and Criminal Justice. She
has written a number of books on penal matters, and in
1999 she became a life peer.

Editor's Introduction

David Conway

A person receives punishment if someone in authority over them deliberately makes them suffer or sustain loss by way of response to the commission of some offence, understood as a breach of law or other rule. More serious offences are commonly termed 'crimes'. To qualify for being so called, an offence must typically involve its perpetrator in knowingly and wilfully having inflicted, or attempted to inflict, suffering or loss upon some third party without authorisation by society.

Since all punishment involves deliberately inflicting suffering or loss, which are both *prima facie* undesirable states, its infliction stands in need of moral justification. Typically, its justification looks back to the past offences for which it is imposed or else forwards to the potential offences its imposition is said to prevent by deterring potential offenders from offending through the fear of thereby becoming liable to it.

Its backward-looking justification locates the rationale for inflicting punishment in the need there is said to be for offenders to be made to suffer or undergo loss in retribution for their offences. On this view, the more serious an offence the more severely does anyone who commits it deserve to be punished. Its forward-looking justification locates the rationale of punishment in its supposed deterrent effect. According to this rationale, its appropriate degree of severity for any given category of offence is whatever is the minimum needed to deter potential offenders from committing offences of this kind.

For those for whom deterrence provides the sole rationale for punishment, were all future crime preventable through introducing some otherwise inert drug into the national water-supply, its introduction would be a better way to avert future crime than punishing past offenders. This is because punishment involves its recipients being subjected to *prima facie* undesirable states. Should its only purpose be achievable without anyone having to undergo any of these states, so much the better.

Many opt for a forward-looking justification for punishment out of the belief it could be deserved by offenders only if they were capable of having chosen *not* to offend, which capacity offenders are then doubted or denied to have. Some deny or doubt offenders have this capacity out of the general belief that all human choice and action is determined by the genetic endowment, environmental conditioning, upbringing and present circumstance of human agents. Others doubt or deny offenders could have chosen not to commit the offences they did on the more circumscribed grounds of supposing them driven by pathological compulsions they were incapable of resisting.

Those who subscribe to a backward-looking justification for punishment do not share either deterministic conception of criminal responsibility. To them, punishment can be deserved because, but only because, offenders were capable of having chosen not to commit their offences, something they are further presumed to have known was required of them by society.

In his essay 'Simple Justice', the celebrated American sociologist Charles Murray provides an uncompromising restatement and defence of the backward-looking, retributive justification of criminal punishment. He also makes an impassioned plea for England to revert to this approach to dealing with convicted offenders, something, he claims, it did until comparatively recently, when those administering its criminal justice system replaced it with a more complex, non-retributive approach.

According to the new approach, when deciding how severely to punish a convicted offender, trial judges in England and Wales now endeavour to take into account a complex range of other considerations besides, or in addition to, the simple one of how grave was the offence of which they have been found guilty. These factors include their degree of likelihood of re-offending, their degree of remorse shown during trial, and the degree of deprivation of their familial background or contemporary social circumstance. Murray takes issue with this more complex non-retributive approach currently favoured by judges. He denies it can be employed, save arbitrarily and hence unsatisfactorily, because it relies on trial judges knowing far more about the offenders before them than could ever be expected. Rather than attempting to employ an approach that, in practice, cannot fail to be employed arbitrarily and hence unsatisfactorily, Murray contends, those responsible for dispensing criminal justice in England would do better to revert to its earlier time-honoured simple retributive approach to punishment. Here, the magnitude of a penalty was determined solely by reference to the gravity of the offence for which it was being imposed.

Murray's essay first appeared in two parts in the *Sunday Times* in January 2004. Civitas is grateful to its editor, John Witherow, for kind permission to reproduce the material. It is accompanied here by comments upon it by several authors who approach it from a number of different perspectives.

Several take issue with it for espousing what in their view is an unduly simple account of what justice demands of society in its treatment of convicted offenders. Christie Davies observes society is never forced to choose in administering punishment between exacting retribution and deterring future offenders. These two objectives, he points out, are not mutually exclusive. In practice, both goals must be sought whenever punishment is imposed to be justified in any given case.

Murray makes a second distinction that Davies firmly endorses. This is a distinction between those whom Murray terms 'Citizens' and 'Outlaws'. The former group is made up of the by-and-large law-abiding majority; the latter group by that relatively small minority of offenders who habitually prey upon members of the former group. Davies suggests 'Outlaw' be turned into a formal legal status whose conferment upon an habitual convicted offender would carry with it forfeiture of certain civil rights and legal protections routinely accorded Citizens, even after Outlaws have served their terms of imprisonment. One legal protection that is currently accorded to all, but which Davies agrees with Murray should be withdrawn anyone whose persistent offending qualifies them for Outlaw status, is their immunity from having their previous criminal record admitted as evidence in court.

Davies rejects, however, as does John Cottingham, a second commentator on Murray's essay, a further suggestion Murray makes. This is that, when on trial for some alleged offence, the past but unproven accusations of similar offences against an accused should be admissible as evidence. Murray claims past accusations be made admissible in alleged cases of rape, since so often the testimony of alleged victims is all there is to go on. Davies disagrees with what Murray proposes. He argues that, unless makers of any accusation against a defendant can be cross-examined by counsel in court, none should be admissible lest they sway a jury into delivering a wrongful conviction. Davies, however, agrees with Murray that not only is it just but positively desirable that society should deprive Outlaws of civil liberties and legal protections routinely accorded Citizens. Doing so, claims Davies, would help society to restore the correct balance between the two groups that it should strive to uphold but which Davies agrees with Murray that England's largely progressive criminal justice élite has of late tilted too far in favour of Outlaws.

In their respective comments, Tom Sorell and John Cottingham both agree with Christie Davies that retributive justice is far more complex a matter than Murray portrays it. Like Davies, Sorell accepts Murray's suggestion that repeat offenders merit being kept under closer surveillance than do ordinary Citizens, even after they have completed their full terms of imprisonment. However, there is much else that Murray proposes in the name of justified retribution that Sorell rejects.

A case in point is Murray's suggestion of how society should respond to victims or would-be victims of serious or violent crime who retaliate against their assailants and kill them in the process. A notorious instance where this happened was when the farmer, Tony Martin, shot dead a burglar who had broken into his farmhouse, an action for which Martin was eventually convicted of manslaughter and imprisoned. Murray claims that in cases where intended victims of violent or serious crime kill their (would-be) assailant in retaliation, they should be considered to have done nothing wrong. Murray's claim is based on his contention that, in committing or attempting to commit the grave offences against which their victims retaliate, these offenders forfeit their right to life.

Sorell disagrees, especially where their societies have abolished capital punishment. He points out that courts might well be entitled to excuse any victims or would-be victims who resort to lethal force, without thereby society condoning or permitting these acts of retaliation in the manner Murray favours. Sorell agree with Murray that criminals should have to serve the full terms of imprisonment of which they become deserving through committing the offences of which they are convicted, no matter how costly it might be for society to arrange this.

John Cottingham, like Tom Sorrell, takes issue with Murray for his seeming willingness to condone in the name of retributive justice acts of violence against (would-be) assailants carried out by their actual or would-be victims. Cottingham agrees with Sorell that such acts might be excusable without being justified. He argues there is need of a moral distinction being drawn between the justified acts of retribution carried out by society against convicted criminals as punishment for their crimes and the unjustifiable, though sometimes excusable, acts of revenge undertaken by victims of violent crime against their (would-be) assailants. In Cottingham's view, what morally distinguishes the former responses from the latter ones, and justifies the former morally speaking, is their being properly authorised, proportionate, and wholly purged of malice or anger. Cottingham claims Murray's choice of emotive examples has the unfortunate effect of tending to blur the force of this distinction.

At a more general level, Cottingham argues that Murray ignores an important aspect of retributive justice by exclusively focusing on only another aspect of it. In consequence, so he claims, even those in favour of a retributive justification of punishment can find themselves in dissent from some of Murray's policy prescriptions. The aspect of retributive justice on which, according to Cottingham, Murray focuses his attention exclusively is society's need to ensure that offenders receive their just deserts through being punished. The aspect of retributive justice that Cottingham claims Murray neglects in consequence is the equally pressing need for society to ensure that non-offenders should not be made to receive punishment for offences of which they are innocent through being wrongfully convicted of them. It is precisely out of concern to safeguard them against these latter forms of injustice that the law accords citizens certain legal protections that many of Murray's proposed policies would threaten out of concern to increase the rate at which offenders are convicted.

In their respective comments on Murray's essay, Baroness Vivian Stern and Rob Allen articulate the concerns of many 'progressives' whose views Murray criticises in it. Baroness Stern voices similar misgivings to those voiced by Cottingham with Murray's proposal that previous convictions of defendants become admissible as evidence in court. Like Cottingham, she thinks their admissibility would risk increasing wrongful convictions to an unacceptably high level.

Baroness Stern also challenges Murray's simple dichotomy between good guys who are deserving of society's protection and bad guys who deserve locking up. She does so by drawing attention to a third group of offenders—those who are mentally disturbed and who are often victims of child abuse with tendencies towards self-harm, Members of this group are often driven to commit or attempt suicide whilst incarcerated. Baroness Stern observes US prisons increasingly house such prisoners who fall into neither of Murray's two categories neatly. She also questions the cost-effectiveness of society incarcerating ever greater numbers of offenders, as Murray suggests, relative to other less expensive, non-custodial responses to crime such as drug-treatment programmes. After drawing attention to the attested correlation between crime and poverty, she suggests that increasing state expenditure on social services in deprived areas might well achieve a greater reduction in crime than increasing imprisonment. She also questions whether public opinion is quite as retributivist and un-progressive as Murray claims it to be.

Rob Allen shares many of the same concerns as Baroness Stern, including what they consider to be the likely high social and financial cost of increasing English rates of incarceration to current US levels. Allen's chief concern with Murray's simple approach to criminal justice, however, is what he considers to be Murray's failure to appreciate sufficiently the complexity of the factors that give rise to criminal behaviour and of which society needs to take full account in determining how best to respond to it. Allen agrees with Baroness Stern that the large proportion of drug addicts and mentally ill among offenders makes their treatment a more humane and effective way to respond to their offending than their imprisonment.

In addition, Allen voices three further misgivings with Murray's views. First, he argues, Murray's simple dichotomy between Citizens and Outlaws ignores how disproportionately serious offenders are drawn from the ranks of the poor, ill-educated, abused, and mentally ill. For society to treat these offenders as Outlaws, as Murray suggests, rather than in need of society's help makes their reform more difficult. Second, Allen contends that Murray's claim that society has a moral duty to punish offenders, and that this should be the primary purpose of sentencing, ignores its other potential functions. In addition to exacting retribution and seeking to prevent crime through offender-incapacitation and deterrence, the sentences handed out to convicted offenders can, and, in Allen's view, should, seek their reform and rehabilitation, as well as encourage them to make reparation towards their victims. What justice demands in relation to sentencing becomes far more complex a matter than Murray portrays it, claims Allen, once its other potential purposes are taken into account. Finally, echoing here a point also made by Baroness Stern, Allen denies public attitudes to crime to be as simple and unequivocally retributivist as Murray presents them as being.

That convicted offenders should be made to provide victims with full restitution for the damage and loss they cause them, rather than simply suffer punishment or else be treated with leniency as themselves victims of illness or hardship, is the central claim made by J.C. Lester in his comments on Murray's essay. Lester offers a view of how much restitution assailants owe their victims for the harms they cause them. It involves reference to a notion Lester terms the 'risk-multiplier', by which he means the additional loss victims of crime sustain over and above any damage or loss to life, limb, or property. The extra loss they suffer consists in the risk they sustain that this loss or damage might go without restitution by their assailant escaping apprehension for their crime. The greater the risk a crime might escape apprehension the greater harm does their victim suffer at their hands and the more their assailant owes them as restitution.

Lester approaches Murray's essay from an extreme libertarian perspective which supposes competing private agencies can and would achieve criminal justice for their clients more efficiently and equitably than can states. Lester explains how, in the kind of stateless society he favours, offenders might be forced to provide their victims with restitution for their offences.

By focusing on the restitution offenders owe their victims, Lester argues, the libertarian approach to crime he favours provides a more just and attractive response to crime than both the simple retribution favoured by Murray, as well as the greater leniency towards criminals called for by Murray's more 'progressive' critics.

The re-publication here of Murray's essay together with the diverse range of comments on it by his several critics forms a timely intervention in the current national debate on how society can and should respond to currently high and seemingly ever-increasing levels of violent and other serious crime. It should be of value to students and teachers of criminology as well as policy-makers.

Simple Justice

Charles Murray

1

England's Reluctant Crime Fighters

The story was told by an American student named Valerie Ruppel who had returned from a semester at her college's London extension. Two days after her group reached England, a policewoman came to South Kensington to brief them on how to keep themselves safe. I pick up her account in her own words:

> Her first question was to the women, 'How many of you brought Mace?' Three girls raised their hands. She told us we couldn't use it, shouldn't even carry it, it was illegal.
>
> Had any of us brought any other type of weapon, such as a knife? Several of the men in our group indicated that they carried pocket knives. She told us to leave them at home too.
>
> Then she instructed us on how to properly be a victim. If we were attacked, we were to assume a defensive posture, such as raising our hands to block an attack. The reason (and she spelled it out in no uncertain terms) was that if a witness saw the incident and we were to attempt to defend ourselves by fighting back, the witness would be unable to tell who the aggressor was. However, if we rolled up in a ball, it would be quite clear who the victim was.[1]

This is the police talking—the police, the ones who are supposed to line up on the side of the good guys. If Mace is illegal, why not tell the women what legal substances they could carry (pepper spray or perhaps a particularly irritating hairspray) and add helpfully, 'It works best if you go for the eyes'? Pocket knives are legal. Why tell the men to leave them at home? The truly puzzling advice was to roll up in a ball if attacked so that a witness could tell who the victim was. Are we to believe that when a man has been seen grappling with a woman in the street, it's going be a problem for the police to determine who the aggressor was? Most of all: Why are police giving this kind of mealy-mouthed advice in a country that is supposed to be in the midst of a war on crime?

Following the English press from across the Atlantic, I knew that horror stories about violent crime are a staple of the daily press and that Middle England's unhappiness about the police and courts is widespread. I knew that Tony Blair came to office after a campaign in which 'Tough on crime, tough on the causes of crime' had been one of his most popular themes, and that he subsequently sent Parliament a blizzard of proposals, more than 40 Bills out of the Home Office in the last six years. I knew that the government's rhetoric has been aggressive, with David Blunkett sounding as ready to throw the book at criminals as Michael Howard ever had. And the police still want people to roll up in a ball if attacked?

Two worlds of English crime

It wasn't just Ms Ruppel's story that made me wonder how much the behaviour of the English criminal justice system has actually changed. When I first looked at England's crime problem for the *Sunday Times* in 1989, I was assured that the rise in crime was a statistical illusion and that the public was in a 'moral panic' for no good reason.[2] Fifteen years later, I read the government's upbeat emphasis on the decrease in property crime shown by all sources and the drop in violent crime shown by the *British Crime Survey*, playing down the continued increases in violent crime shown by police statistics. Moral panic is still a favourite explanation of the public's continued concern about crime, now blamed on the tabloid press.

Meanwhile, everything I read about the people who run the criminal justice system indicates that they are waging guerrilla war against their political masters. The newly appointed Director of Public Prosecutors calls David Blunkett's proposals for stricter sentencing policy 'grotesque,' and laments that the politicians pander to public opinion. Sir David Ramsbotham, the retired chief inspector of prisons, publishes a book attacking the increased use of incarceration. The Sentence Advisory Panel, a Home Office committee operating independently of the Home Secretary, recommends community sentences for muggings that don't physically injure the victim. Even the Prime Minister's wife,

Cherie Booth QC, goes on record about the 'urgent need' to find alternatives to prison.

The bench adds its considerable prestige to the battle against the government's reforms. Twenty Lord Justices of Appeal gather to plot strategy for foiling the government's proposed changes to sentencing laws. Lord Ackner, a retired Law Lord, recommends that judges ignore sentencing guidelines even if they are passed. The nation's most senior judge, Lord Woolf, issues broadside after broadside against the rising prison population, the get-tough-on-crime mood, and the government's plans for the judiciary.

The Prime Minister and Home Secretary soldier on. 'We've given you the powers,' Blair tells a conference on anti-social behaviour. 'It's time to use them.' David Blunkett blasts magistrates for ignoring new guidelines, telling them that they need to 'stop being social workers and start being enforcers of the law.' But few charged with carrying out the policies seem to think there's a need for them, nor that they are good ideas in any case.

It is as if the criminal justice élites and the public live in different worlds. The criminal justice élites—meaning the people who run the English police, court, and prison systems—live in a world where the real problem is not crime but the government's destructive policies to deal with it. In this world, a judge in Reading accepts a burglar's plea that he acted in self-defence when he injured a policeman trying to arrest him. Meanwhile, members of the public live in a world where civic life in their own neighbourhoods is deteriorating, where they must spend inordinate time and money protecting their property, and where they fear going to places where they didn't used to fear to go. In this world, listeners to BBC Radio 4's *Today* programme, given a chance to nominate the law they would most like to see introduced at the next session of parliament, vote for a law that would grant property owners immunity when defending their homes against intruders.

Two understandings of justice

What's going on? The press accounts suggested to me that the public and criminal justice élites are divided by something more profound than disagreements about what works best. The debate is not really about the comparative recidivism rates of different types of sentences, or whether the annual cost of a prison cell is too high, or whether police should be armed. What really divides the public from the élites, I surmised, are fundamentally different views about the morally right thing to do when dealing with crime. The public view seemed straightforward: the right thing to do is lock up the bad guys and protect the good guys. But the views of the people who are engaged in shaping the English debate about crime were less clear. When I came to England last fall, I set out to explore them.

Justice is a big word. As an entry point for discussing it, I devised a set of hypothetical situations. Seven of the hypotheticals are shown in the accompanying boxes (pp. 7-8). Before reading any further, you might want to decide on your own answers.

One way to score your answers is to add the numbers. The lower your score, the more liberal, compassionate, or soft (depending on one's point of view) your conception of justice. The higher your score, the more tough-minded, punitive, or reactionary (depending on one's point of view) your conception of justice. But for this quiz, the more revealing way to score your answer is to count the number of times you chose the category labelled '3'—the number of times that you did not qualify your answer, did not make room for exceptions, but saw a simple, unambiguous principle at issue. Or to put it another way, to what extent do you think that justice depends on evaluating the complexities of each case? To what extent do you say to hell with the complexities, here are the rules, let's enforce them?

The Hypotheticals

The ground rule. In answering these questions, the only issue is your own conception of justice, whatever that may be. Considerations of practicality, expense, or expediency are irrelevant.

Two men are guilty of a robbery in which the shopkeeper was severely beaten. One comes from a disadvantaged environment and the other comes from an advantaged one. Is it just to punish the advantaged offender more severely?

1   Socioeconomic disadvantage can be a factor in determining culpability, and is justly taken into account in deciding on the punishment.

2   The sentences should be the same, but the treatment after sentence can justly take the nature of the disadvantage into account.

3   Socioeconomic background is irrelevant.

Two men are guilty of a robbery in which the shopkeeper was severely beaten. One offender is remorseful, while the other is unrepentant. Is it just to punish the unrepentant offender more severely?

1   Yes.

2   Yes, within limits.

3   No.

A person knowingly commits a serious crime, but you have infallible foreknowledge that this person will never commit another crime, even if he is not punished. Is it just to use this knowledge to diminish the severity of the punishment?

1   Yes.

2   Yes, within limits.

3   No.

A woman is dragged into an alleyway by an unknown assailant. She sprays Mace in the assailant's eyes, enabling her to escape but causing permanent damage to the assailant's eyesight. Did the woman act rightly? Does the assailant have a just complaint against her?

1   The woman used disproportional force, and the assailant has a just complaint.

2   Technically, the woman used disproportional force, but she should not be prosecuted and the assailant should receive only nominal damages.

3   The woman acted rightly and the assailant has no complaint.

The Hypotheticals

An offender enters a home to burgle it. Upon finding the owner at home, the offender flees into the street. The owner runs after the offender, catches him, and pummels him, causing bruises and contusions. Did the homeowner act rightly? Does the assailant have a just complaint against the homeowner?

1   The homeowner was right in chasing the burglar out of the house, but wrong to pummel him, and the burglar has a just complaint.

2   Technically, the homeowner should have just held the man for the police, but the homeowner should not be prosecuted and the burglar should receive only nominal damages.

3   The homeowner acted rightly and the burglar has no complaint.

A man is on trial for rape. In addition to the evidence involving this particular rape, his record includes four arrests, with circumstantial evidence but no convictions, for rape. Is justice served by letting this additional evidence be part of the trial?

1   A just trial must be limited to the facts of the present case. Admitting evidence from prior cases is unjustly prejudicial.

2   Such evidence may justly be admitted only for convictions or unusually similar modus operandi.

3   Juries should have access to all evidence that is relevant for assessing the likelihood that the defendant is guilty.

A drug is invented that infallibly makes people give truthful answers to questions and has no adverse side effects. Is justice served by compelling all criminal defendants to take the drug and submit to questioning about the alleged offence?

1   No.

2   It would be just to do so, but should be prohibited on other grounds.

3   Yes.

The progressives versus the cops

I will label people with the opposite points of view as the Progressives and the Cops. For the Progressives, justice must deal with a range of behaviours in which we are all sinners of one sort or another. Who doesn't fiddle his income tax, or break traffic laws, or do something else for which he could be prosecuted and convicted if it were known? People end up in the dock for a myriad of reasons, many of them beyond their control. The goal of the criminal justice system is to deal with the behaviour, not to punish it.

For an extreme Progressive, punishment is so irrelevant to justice that the first three hypotheticals are hard to answer. Should an offender with an advantaged background be punished more severely than one from a disadvantaged background. You don't want to 'punish' either one, says Frances Crook, director of the Howard League. 'Punishment doesn't heal the damage and help the victim, nor does it help transform the offender. What you get is more pain. By punishing the disadvantaged offender or the advantaged offender, you're just making things worse. You're increasing the world's experience of pain.' Isn't there any value at all in linking bad behaviour to a punishing consequence? 'Absolutely none.' Things must be done to an offender, for his own good or for the community's, but punishment in itself has no purpose. For a more moderate Progressive, punishment has a place, but a sentence has many other purposes too—rehabilitation, deterrence, a signal to the community, incapacitation—which vary by the specifics of the case, and, hence, so should the sentence.

For Progressives, the right to self-defence is restricted to acts that are proportionate to the danger one is in, and one may certainly not take the law into one's own hands and punish an offender caught in the act. Indeed, preserving the offender's rights is a chief function of the judicial system, as important as preserving the victim's rights or, for that matter, as important as determining guilt or innocence. Admitting evidence of prior crimes prejudices those rights—the court must try a specific offence, not the character of the defendant.

At the other extreme, the Cops see the world with hardly any grey at all. Forget the complications. If you did the crime, take the consequences. Socioeconomic disadvantage? Digby Anderson didn't take long to deal with that one: 'Obviously we aren't interested in their backgrounds in the slightest.' The mugger got Mace in his eyes? Roger Graef shrugged. 'It's an occupational hazard.' The burglar got pummelled? He's lucky that's all he got—another informant remarked tersely that Tony Martin's only mistake was in not arranging for the buckshot to go in the front. Of course the evidence about the prior arrests for rape should be admitted—it is 'absolutely essential' in the view of one of the Cops, echoing the sentiment of others. And if there is a way to get a guilty offender to admit his guilt painlessly, by all means use it—isn't that the point of police work and trials, to find out the truth of what happened?

If you had zero '3's or one '3', consider yourself a bleeding heart. If you had two or three '3's, you are Progressive. Four or five '3's makes you a Cop. Six or seven '3's, and you should be working for the New York City Police Department.

In the fall of 2003, I showed the hypotheticals to some of England's most prominent jurists, politicians, police officials, and advocates for criminal justice reform, plus an unsystematic scattering of others who have taken public positions on these issues. I promised anonymity on specific answers to those whose public positions made it awkward to voice opinions at odds with the existing law or with their party's position.

The Informants

Representatives of the criminal justice éites

David Faulkner. Former director of operational policy in the Prison Service and head of the criminal research and statistics department of the Home Office.

Michael Howard. Currently leader of the Conservative Party, formerly Home Secretary and advocate of greater use of prison as a means of reducing crime.

UNIVERSITIES AT MEDWAY LIBRARY

Christopher Leslie. Parliamentary Under Secretary of State responsible for criminal justice with the Department of Constitutional Affairs.

Oliver Letwin. Former shadow Home Secretary and advocate of greater accountability in prosecution and sentencing.

Sir Charles Pollard. Retired Chief Constable the Thames Valley Police and currently chairman of the Youth Justice Board.

Sir Oliver Popplewell. Retired judge of the High Court.

Sir David Phillips. Director of the National Centre for Policing Excellence, President of the Association of Chief Police Officers, and former Chief Constable of Kent.

Sir David Ramsbotham. Retired Chief Inspector of Prisons.

Professor John Spencer. Professor of Law at Selwyn College, Cambridge, with a long career as consultant in the formulation of criminal justice policy.

Lord Woolf of Barnes. Lord Chief Justice of England and Wales.

The progressive advocates

Rob Allen. Director of the Rethinking Crime and Punishment initiative at the Esmée Fairbairn Foundation, and an advocate of restorative justice.

Paul Cavadino. Chairman of the National Association for the Care and Resettlement of Offenders (NACRO).

Frances Crook. Director of the Howard League for Penal Reform, an advocacy group for promoting alternatives to prison and improved services within prisons.

Juliet Lyon. Director of the Prison Reform Trust, an advocacy group for promoting alternatives to prison and improved services within prisons.

Una Padel. Director of the Centre for Crime and Justice Studies of King's College, a research foundation that supports restorative justice and alternatives to prison.

Lucy Russell. Director of the 'SmartJustice' campaign and an advocate of community sentencing as an alternative to prison.

The others

Jonathan Aitken. Former Tory cabinet minister, subsequently imprisoned for perjury in 1999, now a director of the Christian charity Prison Fellowship International.

Digby Anderson. Director of the Social Affairs Unit, an independent think tank, and author of numerous books on the deterioration of English civil society.

Norman Brennan. A policeman and detective for 24 years, now Head of the Victims of Crime Trust, an advocacy group for victims.

Frank Field. Labour MP from Birkenhead and former minister of welfare reform.

Roger Graef. Film and television producer, and creator of several important documentaries relating to policing and alternatives to incarceration.

David Green. Director of Civitas, an independent think tank, and frequent commentator on criminal justice policy.

Simon Jenkins. Columnist for *The Times* and critic of the increased use of incarceration as a means of dealing with crime.

Tony Martin. Farmer convicted of manslaughter and incarcerated for four years for killing a youth who had burgled his home.

Who were the Cops and who were the Progressives? In one respect, the results were predictable. Six of my informants were leading advocates for liberal penal reform. None of them gave more than two answers that could be categorised as '3's. No surprise there.

Now consider the public officials who hold or have recently held important positions related to criminal justice. There were ten of them: three politicians, two judges, two senior police officials, a senior civil servant in the Home Office, a senior administrator of the prison service, and an academician who has been an influential advisor on legal policy.

The results were much more extreme than I would have predicted. Sir David Phillips, president of the Association of Chief Police Officers, qualified as a Cop. *None* of the other nine did. All were Progressives of one variety or another. Four of them gave just one answer that could be classified as a '3', four of them gave two '3's, and one gave three '3's. There were a few more '3's and a few more '2's among the public officials than among the reformers, but so few that there's no way to get around the basic conclusion: The profiles of answers from people who have devoted their lives to advocacy of progressive reforms were nearly indistinguishable from the profiles of people who are part of the criminal justice élites.

These people were chosen for interviews because of their prominence in the debate, not as a random sample. The results should not be interpreted as statistically representative. But there's no reason to think that the sample was weighted toward the left. Two of the three politicians were Tories. David Ramsbotham came to his post after a distinguished military career. Charles Pollard may not be a Cop, but he was a career policeman. Retired Judge Oliver Popplewell and Professor John Spencer scarcely qualify as wild-eyed liberals. David Faulkner worked for 30 years as career civil servant in the Home Office. Only Lord Woolf has a long history of published views that would clearly make him a Progressive. As a group, these representatives of the criminal justice élites are likely to be a bit more conservative than the average.

And yet all but one were Progressives in their view of justice. How can this be, when the group would appear to be so politically diverse? I think the answer is that they all took the ground rule seriously: 'In answering these questions, the only issue is your own conception of justice, whatever that may be. Considerations of practicality, expense, or expediency are irrelevant.' Liberal or conservative, they talked about the essence of justice as they saw it, and that essence included many complications and qualifications that prevented most of their answers from being classified as '3's. Thus one public figure among my informants, politically conservative, answered the first hypothetical by saying, 'It is *just*'—his emphasis—'to take into account disadvantages which have contributed to the bringing of a particular offender to a particular point in his life when he committed that offence, and that would in many circumstances lead you to impose a slightly more lenient sentence than you otherwise would.' The same man found it just to take remorse and likelihood of re-offending into account, for reasons having nothing to do with his support of strict law enforcement, but with the underlying conception of justice in which he believes. David Blunkett is certainly not soft on crime, but might very well be defined as a Progressive by his answers (he wasn't available for an interview), as might Tony Blair. My point is not that the criminal justice élites are uniformly soft on crime in practice; rather, that just about everyone in the élites has bought into a broadly similar philosophical view of justice—a view that sees a just sentence as a complicated balancing of the nature of the offence, the particulars of the offender's situation, protection of the rights of the offender, and concern with the effect that a sentence will have on the offender.

The specific policies of those who share a Progressive view of justice can vary widely. People like Lord Woolf resist the government's reforms ferociously, thinking that they are profoundly wrong. People like Michael Howard and David Blunkett urge increased use of imprisonment—but that practical policy, aimed specifically at reducing the crime rate, is consistent with a view of the role of prison that would permit '1' answers on the first three hypotheticals. What I have not heard people in the criminal justice élites espouse, including the toughest reformers, are positions such as, 'The prison population should depend on the number of people who commit serious crimes, and if that means tripling the prison population, so be it.' I have not heard them say 'Whether prison rehabilitates people is irrelevant in deciding whether an offender should go to prison.' I have not heard them say 'Tony Martin did nothing wrong.' As far as I can determine, not just from my interviews but from the published commentary on the government's policies, the number of criminal justice élites who hold such views is close to zero. In such an environment, any get-tough policy is operating against the wind. Many of the originators of the policy see themselves as engaged in regrettable necessities and, given the alternative, would take a less harsh approach. Large numbers—by my estimate, a large majority—of the senior administrators of tough policies oppose them outright.

At this point, I suspect some substantial portion of the my readers wonders how anyone could object to the prevailing élite wisdom. Won't any reasonable person agree that sometimes a person's background is so disadvantaged that it has to be taken into account? That remorse should be taken into account? That the likelihood of re-offending should be taken into account? That offenders don't give up their rights when they commit a crime? That criminal defendants must be protected from unproven allegations of past offences? That pummelling the burglar may be understandable, but still should be against the law? Or, to put it more bluntly, I can hear a substantial number of readers asking: What kind of simple-minded reactionaries gave a majority of answers that I classify as '3'?

Well, Tony Martin for one, who during a long conversation near his home in Norfolk gave me a poignant account of what it was like to be at the centre of one of the defining cases of the criminal justice debate. But Tony Martin would take that position, wouldn't he? Norman Brennan, the director of the Victims of Crime Trust, qualified as a Cop, but he is in fact a retired street cop, and he runs an advocacy group that is as far to the right on the crime debate as the Howard League is to the left. What else would one expect?

David Green, director of Civitas, and Digby Anderson, director of the Social Affairs Unit are Cops. But that too is predictable—they run independent think tanks and write books about the importance of the two-parent family and civility and traditional British values. Those books evince formidable erudition, so the 'simple-minded' label is hard to pin on them, but their attitudes toward justice will naturally be a bit reactionary.

Explaining away Jonathan Aiken's answers poses a bit more of a problem. The former Tory cabinet minister, imprisoned for perjury, is now a committed Christian and an active supporter of restorative justice—so active that I nearly classified him with the professional advocates of progressive reform. And yet he qualified as a Cop ('I haven't gone soft on crime just because I was in prison,' he remarked as he completed his answers). Roger Graef also would seem to be a natural Progressive—he has made television documentaries critical of police practices and in favour of alternatives to prison—but a majority of his answers were straightforward '3's.

The other Cop, as extreme a Cop as anyone I interviewed, was Frank Field—the same Frank Field who has been representing an archetypal working-class Labour constituency in Birkenhead for a quarter of a century and was Tony Blair's minister for welfare reform. He has written a number of influential books on public policy, all rooted in the political philosophy of the left. And yet there he sat, running through the hypotheticals, seldom requiring more than a sentence or two to render his crisp and sometimes pungent opinions—and nearly all of them were '3's.

The Cops among my informants were not such a homogeneous group, and brushing them off as unreflective or reactionaries can't be done if you've talked to them. Their view of justice is simple, not simple minded —a profoundly important distinction.

2

The Case for Simple Justice

The false promises of progressive justice

The progressive view of justice has qualities that people with high IQs and advanced degrees tend to like: It is nuanced and uses complicated explanations for human behaviour. It also has the quality that tends to make such theories disastrous as public policy: What can be put into practice bears no resemblance to the promises of the theory.

The reality is that no one is smart enough to get justice right when attempting to balance the factors that progressive justice tries to balance. Consider how hard it is for parents to be sure whether a misbehaving child needs an explanation with a hug, a stern warning, or a lesson that won't soon be forgotten. Now compare how much parents know about their own children with how little judges know about convicted offenders who appear before them for sentencing.

The judge has seen the offender for a matter of hours at most, more likely a matter of minutes. He may have read a sentencing report on the defendant, often sketchy, often factually wrong. The judge is then supposed to assess whether the offender feels genuine remorse and whether the offender is likely to re-offend. How? Everyone who stands before the judge is highly motivated to say whatever the judge wants to hear and be whatever the judge wants him to be. The better the criminal, the better the act will be. The judge is supposed to be able to see through all that and accurately assess whether the offender is really, truly sorry for what he did and is going to change his ways. It is an absurd premise. Even if the judge succeeds in making this problematic decision and correctly decides that an offender is remorseful, that doesn't mean that the offender will stop offending. Two other characteristics of criminals are impulsiveness and a short time horizon. Offenders can be really, truly sorry for what they did today and be back on the streets doing it again a week from now. As police and probation officers will tell you, it happens all the time. The judge is supposed to decide whether the offender will respond better to a community sentence or to prison. How? Individual case histories of offenders reveal every kind of response, from the offender who is set straight by a tough prison sentence to the one who sees the errors of his ways through apologising to his victim. A judge has to guess. I know that judges prefer to call it the use of judicial discretion, not guessing—but guessing is what it really amounts to. Making matters worse, the guess usually reflects not the unique characteristics of the defendant and the offence, but the judge's personal ideology.

Everything I have said about judges applies equally to the people in the Crown Prosecution Service who are making decisions about whether to plea-bargain, drop charges or bring a case to trial. For practical purposes, the question of whether the justice system should take personalities, background, remorse or predictions about future behaviour into account when deciding what should be done to an offender is moot. Whether or not it should, it can't. Prosecutors and judges cannot be that smart about the parade of offenders who come before them. Progressive justice does not do—*cannot* do—what it claims to do.

Retributive justice

The simple alternative to progressive justice is called retributive justice. It is the modern version of the systems of justice that came into being at the dawn of human history, and it is based on the same reasoning.

The primal function of a system of justice is to depersonalise revenge. The agreement, perhaps the most ancient of all agreements that make it possible for communities to exist, is that the individual will take his complaint to the community. In return, the community will exact the appropriate retribution—partly on behalf of the wronged individual, but also to express the community's moral values. Justice means retribution through punishment and upholding the supremacy of the good members of the community over the bad ones.

The word *retribution* is jarring to the modern sensibility. Someone who wants retribution is harking back to the bad old days of an eye for an eye, we think. Retribution is something that civilized societies ought to rise above. The victim's desire for retribution is atavistic and unworthy.

Is it? As a way of testing your own views, consider a thought experiment that Immanuel Kant posed two centuries ago. He imagined an island society that is to disband tomorrow. Its citizens must decide whether a murderer awaiting execution should be executed. (If you're against the death penalty, substitute some other suitable punishment.) Executing him will have no expedient benefit for the members of the society. It will certainly have no benefit for the prisoner. We may assume that if the prisoner is released, he will not kill again. The *only* purpose of the punishment is retribution. Should the murderer be executed? Kant says yes, that 'the last murderer remaining in prison must first be executed so that everyone will duly receive what his actions are worth'.[1] Your own answer should give you some sense of whether you are a retributivist at heart.

This way of looking at the function of justice has a distinguished intellectual pedigree (an excellent recent treatment is Michael S. Moore's *Placing Blame*, weighing in at 849 pages),[2] but the principle itself is deeply ingrained in most people's sense of the rightness of things. It feels instinctively wrong when someone does something bad and gets away with it. When we say that someone 'gets away with it,' we mean that the person suffers no punishment, or too little punishment.

Perhaps the case of murder is too easy—one can think that retributive justice is appropriate for such an extreme crime, but not for lesser ones. Let me offer another thought experiment, this one inspired by my interview with Una

Padel, the director the Centre for Crime and Justice
Studies, a research foundation that advocates alternatives
to prison and restorative justice. A fortnight before we
talked, her 13-year-old daughter had been mugged. If the
muggers could be brought to account (they cannot, even
though the daughter knows who they are), what would
Padel have in mind for them? True to her principles, she
does not want the muggers jailed. 'I remain angry with
them, but I don't want anything horrible to happen to
them,' she said. 'I want them to stop robbing people, that's
the bottom line. ... In an ideal world I would like them to be
made aware of the impact they've actually had on my
daughter and, ideally, apologise.'

Una Padel is no dewy-eyed *naïf*. She has dealt with
criminals for years and is easily as knowledgeable and
unsentimental as any judge who is likely to try the case. It's
her own daughter that has suffered the harm. The thought
experiment: If she had the power, would Una Padel be
morally entitled to substitute a sentence that does not
punish the muggers for one that does? I will even stipulate
that her sentence inspires genuine remorse in the muggers
and that they stop mugging (generous stipulations indeed).
Would justice be done if Una Padel had her way?

The principles of retributive justice say no. Justice does
not consist of successful therapy. It consists of just deserts.
The just desert for terrorising a 13-year-old and robbing her
must entail punishment, whether or not the muggers
already feel bad about what they've done and whether or
not they will do it again. Una Padel and her daughter have
the moral right and perhaps a spiritual obligation to forgive
the muggers. They do not have the moral right to abrogate
the community's obligation to punish wrong behaviour.

These two thought experiments will have conveyed the
flavour of retributive justice. To spell out its core tenets:
*The necessary and sufficient justification for punishing
criminals is that they did something for which they deserve
punishment.* 'Something' refers to the behaviours that
society has defined as offences. 'Deserve' means that the
offenders are culpable—morally responsible. *Society not
only has the right but the duty to punish culpable offenders.*

Punishing people for acts deserving of punishment is not just a sentencing option. The moral responsibility of the offender imposes on society the obligation to punish.

That's it. Nothing about rehabilitation, remorse, or socioeconomic disadvantage. Nothing about the bad effects that the punishment might have on the offender or, for that matter, its good effects. The purpose of a sentence is punishment. When a system fails to punish culpable offenders, it has failed, full stop. It is unjust.

Before rejecting retributivism out of hand as far too harsh, you should realise that you can be a retributivist and still be against disproportionate punishments. You can oppose the death penalty, for example, or think that the appropriate punishment for painting graffiti on a park bench is not a jail term, but being forced to scrub graffiti from ten park benches. Being a retributivist does not mean you must give up on rehabilitation. Add all the educational and therapeutic services you want to the sentence—as long as the sentence itself constitutes a punishment. You can be a retributivist and still be a civil libertarian of sorts. A just system requires that culpability be judged correctly, which means that criminal justice procedures should protect the innocent.

Citizens and Outlaws

But if retributive justice is not as harsh as it may first appear, neither is it warm and fuzzy. Before you decide that you are a retributivist after all, you have to decide what you think of this collateral view of crime and justice that is necessary to make retributivism work: For practical purposes, society can be divided into Citizens and Outlaws. In conflicts between them, the law should favour the Citizens.[3]

The progressive view of justice vehemently rejects this notion, starting instead from the premise I mentioned earlier: we are all sinners. Some of us pad expense accounts while others mug pensioners—both acts are thefts of different types. People fit on a continuum, not into black and white categories, and justice should reflect that continuum.

In defending a dichotomy between Citizens and Outlaws, I am allying myself with an old English legal maxim: because there is twilight does not mean there is neither night nor day. We are all sinners in God's eyes, but the everyday world contains millions of decent, law-abiding people—the people whom I label *Citizens*—who are different in kind from a much smaller number of people whom I label *Outlaws*. Perhaps Citizens pad their expense accounts, but they never come close to killing, wounding, robbing, burgling, or raping—the elemental predatory acts. The person who does kill, wound, rob, burgle, or rape has stepped over a line and become an Outlaw. While he is in a state of Outlawry, he has lost many rights that Citizens enjoy.

During the actual commission of the crime, the Outlaw's rights have nearly disappeared. The hypotheticals about the use of Mace by the young woman and the pummelling of the fleeing burglar speak to this point. The extreme view is that a mugger has no cause for complaint if the young woman not only sprays him with Mace, but pulls out a handgun. The burglar has no complaint if the homeowner pulls out a shotgun and shoots him as he attempts to flee. In both cases, the Outlaw has caused his own wounding or death—if he had chosen to be a neighbour instead of a predator, he would have gone utterly unharmed. Other retributivists take a less wide-open view of the conditions under which lethal force is justified, but the common principle is that criminals in the act of committing a crime are taking their chances. Victims are not expected to respond 'proportionally' to being victimised.

The state of being an Outlaw also implies reduced rights during the judicial process. The principle to be upheld is that the judicial process is not a game, but a solemn search for the truth. The objective of the judicial process is to know as much as possible about all that can assist in determining the truth.

The hypothetical about the infallible truth serum is relevant here. Rules against self-incrimination make sense not because confessions are a bad thing, but because states have had an ugly habit of coercing inaccurate confessions. The only way to prevent coercion has been to make sweeping rules against forced self-incrimination. That has been a practical necessity, not to be confused with an offender's 'right' to hide incriminating evidence about himself. People who are accused of offences have a right not to be tortured —that's the extent of it, and the only legitimate argument is about the nature of torture. Some retributivists will see an aggressive verbal interrogation as a form of torture, to be constrained by regulation; others will set a looser standard. But if an infallible truth serum were invented, with no side effects, and was used only to question people about the specific allegation for which they have been arrested, almost any retributivist would agree that justice is served by compelling its use. A retributivist might decide to prohibit the use of the truth serum on other grounds (it gives the state too much power, for example), but not on grounds of justice. Forcing defendants to give DNA samples is an analogous resource already with us.

Should evidence of prior arrests be excluded from a trial? If justice is a game, yes. If justice is a search for truth, no. In every human endeavour other than justice, we take it for granted that arriving at the truth is aided by assembling as much relevant information as possible. The employer hiring someone for an important post does not limit his assessment to the impression he gets from the job interview, but tries as best he can to discover how the applicant performed on previous jobs. A woman whose husband comes home with lipstick on his collar and a plausible explanation takes his prior history into account before deciding whether to believe him. Only the criminal justice system has the wacky notion that data about prior behaviour should be excluded in deciding upon a person's guilt or innocence.

The hypothetical uses rape as its topic because rape so vividly illustrates the importance of the prior record. Rape almost never has witnesses and often leaves no physical evidence that discriminates rape from consensual sex. In today's world, even lack of previous acquaintance is not decisive—if a man and woman meet each other in a pub and leave together, her claim of rape does not acquire credibility just because it was the first night they met. And so the jury in such a case has a daunting problem. Rape is among the most serious offences, and should be punished severely. Consensual sex is no offence at all, and sending a man to prison for it is a profound miscarriage of justice. Suppose that you are on the jury, there is no physical evidence, and the accuser and defendant are both plausible witnesses. It is a coin flip—but you do not have the option of opting out. You have a 50-50 chance of committing a terrible injustice. Now suppose you are told that four other women have independently filed complaints of date rape against this same man over the last few years even though none of those complaints resulted in a conviction. It is no longer a coin flip. The chances of a terrible miscarriage of justice have plummeted.

Rape is the archetypal case, but it is not different in kind from burglary, robbery, or any other crime. A witness has picked out the defendant on a burglary charge from a lineup, let us say, but the light was bad and you, the juror, are not willing to estimate the likelihood of a correct identification at 100 per cent—90 per cent perhaps, but not 100 per cent. You are then told that the defendant has never been arrested for anything, holds a steady job, and is a faithful member of the church choir. Does that knowledge make you back off from treating the witness's identification of the defendant as decisive and lead you to have reasonable doubt? It may well do. And what you have heard— appropriately and usefully—is in fact information about the defendant's 'prior record'. It would be just as appropriate and useful to know that the defendant had prior arrests for criminal behaviour.

The only reason that excluding evidence from prior arrests make sense is if we don't trust jurors' good sense. The criterion of 'beyond a reasonable doubt' gives jurors no choice but to work with probabilities. They must combine many different types of evidence, none of them absolutely conclusive, and come up with their best estimate of an overall probability of guilt. The importance of prior record can vary widely. If the defendant's prior record consisted of one arrest for a misdemeanour ten years ago, that record should be irrelevant to the jury's calculation of probabilities. If the prior record consists of four recent arrests using a *modus operandus* identical to the present case, it should be extremely important. Why not rely upon jurors being able to make such distinctions in the same way that they make such distinctions in other aspects of their daily lives? On this point, I suspect that just about everyone who has served on a jury and has discovered later that evidence was kept from them has had the same reaction that I had when it happened to me: Fury that the system had impeded me and my fellow jurors from doing a difficult job as fairly as possible.

If we admit prior criminal record in testimony, are we not conflating the defendant's character with his guilt for the crime in question? In the case of defendants with many prior arrests and convictions, yes—and this is a virtue of admitting prior records, not a defect. One of the most consistent findings about crime around the world is that a small proportion of offenders commit a very large proportion of the crimes. Divinely accurate retributive justice would not punish for the one burglary out of dozens when the burglar got caught, but for the aggregate harm that the burglar has done. Judging whether an offender in the dock is an habitual offender is useful in deciding on the probability of guilt in the present case and essential to deciding on the severity of the punishment. A record of many prior arrests is an indicator, more reliable than most, that should feed into both judgments.

All of the issues I have treated so sketchily raise genuinely difficult problems that need to be considered at length. I will not try to do so here, but state the principle that I believe should be taken to that lengthy consideration: In making judgments about the benefits and risks of alternative policies, the playing field is not supposed to be level. Citizens get preference.

As the debate stands, Citizens are in effect held hostage to threats by the Outlaws ('If you put me in prison, I'll just become a worse criminal'). As the debate stands, the legal protections needed for an innocent defendant are treated as if they are identical with the legal protections needed for a guilty defendant (they aren't). As the debate stands, nobody is supposed to mention the obvious: Everything good in

English life is produced by the Citizens. That they may go about their lives freely and in peace is the highest goal that government can serve.

Implementing retributive justice

I observed earlier that progressive justice makes promises it cannot keep. Our ability to fine-tune our diagnoses and treatments for criminal behaviour is so limited that nobody knows how to do what the principles of progressive justice requires. In contrast, retributive justice is not only simple in concept, it is simple to implement.

Require the legislature to set punishments that are commensurate with the gravity of the various offences. Cosmically accurate calibrations of wrongfulness are not necessary here, only a system that reflects the society's consensus through a responsive democratic process. Eras and societies treat the same act differently. Retributive justice requires that at any point in time, offences and their commensurate punishments be defined.

Focus criminal justice resources on the most serious offences. Once again, the definition of terms—'most serious', in this case—is to be based on the society's consensus. The point is that all crimes are not treated equally by the police, courts, and prisons. When choices must be made, the crimes that society condemns the most severely are the ones that get the most attention by the police and prosecutors, and those convicted of such offences get first call on the limited number of prison cells.

Use all the evidence about an offender in deciding on guilt and on the severity of sentence. In addition to opening up the rules of evidence, discussed earlier, this principle implies choosing juries that know the most about the defendant and are best able to process complex information. Jury selection rules that tend to encourage the selection of the least informed and least educated members of the community are self-defeating.

Limit the ability of judges to depart from the prescribed penalty. The operative word is *limit*. A variety of strategies can permit judges to take the specific circumstances of the crime and offender into account, varying the sentence within a limited range, yet restrain them from imposing their own views about the defendant or about the sociology of crime and punishment. The United States offers a sampling of such strategies that have been implemented at the federal and state levels during the last two decades.

Administer the punishment. Run the prisons properly and make sure that community sentences are carried out as pre-scribed—not administratively easy tasks, but straightfor-ward and do-able.

Implementing retributive justice is simple, but expensive. In modern England, the only authentic punishment for serious felonies is imprisonment. To implement retributive justice would mean an increase in the prison population that dwarfs anything that any politician, including the ones who are most vehemently anti-crime, is prepared to counte-nance.

To see just how extraordinary the increase in the prison population would be, consider England as of 1954. If you divide the number of persons convicted of robbery who were incarcerated that year by the number of robberies reported to the police during that year, the ratio in 1954 was 1 to 3. In 2002, the comparable ratio was 1 to 22. For burglary in a dwelling, the ratio was 1 to 18 in 1954 compared to 1 to 59 in 2002. For felonious wounding, the ratio was 1 to 5 in 1954 compared to 1 to 12 in 2002.

Because misunderstanding of this issue is so common, I should emphasise that the leniency of judges after a conviction is a minor reason for these contrasting numbers. Judges are almost as tough on convicted offenders in contemporary England as they were in 1954.[4] Leniency resides in the ways that bringing an accused to trial has been made so difficult and time-consuming, and is reflected in the large proportions of cleared-up cases that are not prosecuted as felonies and in the decreasing clear-up rates for serious crimes.

The bottom line is staggering. If England today impris-oned the same ratio of people relative to the number of the most serious offences (murder, attempted murder, serious woundings, rape, burglary, and robbery) that it imprisoned in 1954, the English prison population in 2004 would be of the order of 290,000, almost four times the current prison population that is causing such a stir.[5] The note describes ways in which this specific number could be too high or too low, but, even with the most conservative assumptions, Britain cannot implement a system that consistently punishes criminals for the most serious offences without more than doubling, probably tripling, and perhaps quadrupling the prison population that is already thought by the criminal justice élites to be too high. The changes in practice produced by the reforms of the last half dozen years have been trivial when the frame of reference is English criminal justice as it used to be.

Using that frame of reference is a good idea. The view of justice I have advocated must seem radical and barbarically punitive to many readers. But that's the system England used to have—and not in the Dark Ages, but at the beginning of the reign of Elizabeth II. England still practiced retributive justice back in 1954, although nobody called it that. It was simply British justice, the only kind that crossed anyone's mind.

It worked. In the first half of the twentieth century, England had one of the freest societies ever created, and at the same time one with such extraordinary little crime that the civility of English life was an international cliché. The professionalism of English police and the fairness of English courts set standards for the world. It was not a perfect system, but perfection is not what complex governmental systems can aspire to. By any realistic measure, English criminal justice was superb. Its philosophical core was what I have been calling retributive justice, applied consistently and without apology. Isn't it time for its return?

Postscript

The *Sunday Times* Readers
and the Hypotheticals

Before the newspaper version of these articles ran, I suggested to the *Sunday Times* editors that they encourage readers to give their own answers to the hypotheticals either through letters to the editor or on the *Sunday Times* website. But I urged that some background questions also had to be included—at a minimum, age, sex, and occupation. My reasoning was that a random sample of the affluent, well-educated *Sunday Times* readership would include a higher percentage of Progressives on the crime question than the nation as a whole. Perhaps I underestimated the conservatism of the *Sunday Times*'s readership, but my experience during the interviewing and other conversations in the autumn had consistently indicated that mainstream Tories are not that different from mainstream Labourites in their view of the hypotheticals. Highly educated people are drawn to nuance and complexity whether they are of the left or right, and the '3' answers give no room for nuance or complexity. When I looked at the website after the article appeared and discovered that the *Sunday Times* had not included any such questions, I was sure that the results would be uninterpretable, and, to a casual reader, misleading.

The results, shown below, amazed me. The responses were extraordinarily weighted toward the '3' answers that define the Cops—the same '3' answers that the criminal justice élites I interviewed so seldom gave. For six out of the seven hypotheticals, the '3' had an outright majority, once amounting to more than 80 per cent of the responses.

Total number of responses: 1,441   % of
                                               respondents

*Two men are guilty of a robbery in which the shopkeeper was
severely beaten. One comes from a disadvantaged environment
and the other comes from an advantaged one. Is it just to
punish the advantaged offender more severely?*

1   Socioeconomic disadvantage can be a factor in determin-
     ing culpability, and is justly taken into account in decid-
     ing on the punishment   5

2   The sentences should be the same, but the treatment
     after sentence can justly take the nature of the disadvan-
     tage into account   33

3   Socioeconomic background is irrelevant   62

*Two men are guilty of a robbery in which the shopkeeper was
severely beaten. One offender is remorseful, while the other is
unrepentant. Is it just to punish the unrepentant offender more
severely?*

1   Yes   16

2   Yes, within limits   45

3   No   40

*A person knowingly commits a serious crime, but you have
infallible foreknowledge that this person will never commit
another crime, even if he is not punished. Is it just to use this
knowledge to diminish the severity of the punishment?*

1   Yes   7

2   Yes, within limits   36

3   No   57

*A woman is dragged into an alleyway by an unknown assail-
ant. She sprays Mace in the assailant's eyes, enabling her to
escape but causing permanent damage to the assailant's eyesight. Did the woman act rightly? Does the assailant have a
just complaint against her?*

1   The woman used disproportional force, and the assailant
     has a just complaint   3

2   Technically, the woman used disproportional force, but
     she should not be prosecuted and the assailant should
     receive only nominal damages   15

3   The woman acted rightly and the assailant has no com-
     plaint   82

An offender enters a home to burgle it. Upon finding the owner at home, the offender flees into the street. The owner runs after the offender, catches him, and pummels him, causing bruises and contusions. Did the homeowner act rightly? Does the assailant have a just complaint against the homeowner?

1   The homeowner was right in chasing the burglar out of the house, but wrong to pummel him, and the burglar has a just complaint   13

2   Technically, the homeowner should have just held the man for the police, but the homeowner should not be prosecuted and the burglar should receive only nominal damages   29

3   The homeowner acted rightly and the burglar has no complaint   57

A man is on trial for rape. In addition to the evidence involving this particular rape, his record includes four arrests, with circumstantial evidence but no convictions, for rape. Is justice served by letting this additional evidence be part of the trial?

1   A just trial must be limited to the facts of the present case. Admitting evidence from prior cases is unjustly prejudicial   17

2   Such evidence may justly be admitted only for convictions or unusually similar modus operandi   25

3   Juries should have access to all evidence that is relevant for assessing the likelihood that the defendant is guilty   58

A drug is invented that infallibly makes people give truthful answers to questions and has no adverse side effects. Is justice served by compelling all criminal defendants to take the drug and submit to questioning about the alleged offence?

1   No   11

2   It would be just to do so, but should be prohibited on other grounds   22

3   Yes   68

Nothing too ambitious can be made of these numbers, because we lack specific information on the respondents. But in view of the demographics of the *Sunday Times* readership, the results should at least give pause to those in the élites who try to argue—with breathtaking condescension toward ordinary people—that tough opinions about justice are a matter of a moral panic stirred up by the tabloids.

I am moving into the realm of speculation at this point. But suppose that my characterisation of the criminal justice élites and their view of crime is roughly correct. Suppose that the responses to the unsystematic *Sunday Times* poll are even similar to the results that would be produced by a representative national sample (personally, I judge they are less Cop-like than the results from a nationally representative sample would be). If those two statements are true, the difference between élite and public opinion on this central political issue is a chasm, with implications for political realignment, given an articulate, unapologetic proponent of the Cop viewpoint, that are open-ended.

Commentaries

Not So Simple Justice

Christie Davies

Charles Murray's essay, 'Simple Justice', is just, but it is anything but simple. On the contrary, it raises a very large number of difficult questions. In responding to them, it is necessary first to formulate which questions to consider and then to group answers to them in a coherent way. Accordingly, I have divided my comments into three reasonably self-contained sections, *Retribution, Utility and Simplicity*; *Retribution, Innocence and Rights*; and *Outlaws, Citizens and the Liberal Élite*.

Retribution, utility and simplicity

The need for wrongdoers to be punished in order that they receive their just deserts provides society with a reason to punish them. But are considerations of desert a sufficient reason for punishment, or must they be supplemented by other sorts of reason for punishment in order for it to be justified?

Justifications of punishment usually appeal to both retributive considerations, plus other, more utilitarian forward-looking considerations including the deterrent effects its infliction supposedly has. It is very difficult to see the point of executing Kant's hypothetical murderer were the society which had found him guilty of it about to disband. Retribution is a social act. No society, no retribution. In practice, penalties are always inflicted for a mixture of retributive and utilitarian reasons whose composition varies greatly from one crime to another.

In illustration of this fact, let us look first at two extreme cases. During the First World War, nearly three hundred British soldiers were executed for military offences, mainly desertion. However, as soon as the war ended, these executions ceased, even in the case of those who had already been condemned to death. There was no point. No one believed the soldiers in question were culpable of any crime morally deserving of the death penalty. These sentences had been imposed merely as a deterrent to prevent further acts of desertion. Now that the war was over, this punishment had lost all purpose.

We may contrast this case with the execution of collaborators carried out after World War II in Norway, Belgium and the Netherlands. All of these were countries in which capital punishment had previously been abolished or long in abeyance. The war being over, these executions served no material useful purpose. It would be absurd to suggest they were carried out to deter citizens from collaborating in future possible wars. The fact they took place at all indicates both the strength of the sense of justice of ordinary citizens, as well as the humbug of progressive élites. These good pink men from small neutral *pays fainéants*, who had done away with capital punishment because they held 'civilised' values, now espoused retribution in its purest form. These executions went without protest from left-wing Labour MPs in the British Parliament who were shortly afterwards to attempt to ban capital punishment in Britain. They looked the other way when retribution was being exacted in its severest of forms and then went on to denounce retributive punishment in their own country.

These two post-war situations exhibit the extremes of utilitarian and retributive justifications of punishment. However, in general, we ought, indeed, we are forced, to take both considerations into account. Punishment is not, nor can it ever be, a simple matter. It always involves consideration, at the very least, of both these two different, and at times conflicting, sets of goals and principles.

Most citizens would applaud Charles Murray in rejecting and attempting to refute the almost hegemonic views of Britain's unaccountable progressive élite, but they would do so for a mixture of reasons. Citizens feel that violent muggers and rapists, plus those who hold up shops, post-offices and banks, as well as career domestic burglars and those who gratuitously inflict serious injuries on innocent victims, deserve, upon their being convicted, far more severe punishment than at present they receive. Most of those convicted of such crimes already receive custodial sentences, but citizens think them not long enough. Why are such criminals not serving a decade in jail? Why do not more of them receive the maximum possible terms laid down by parliament?

For them to do so, of course, would result in a very large increase in the numbers of inmates in our prisons and would necessitate the building of many new ones. Why not? It is well established that the cause of the increase of the prison population in Britain lies entirely in the increased number of crimes committed. The ratio of prisoners to those found guilty or cautioned is far lower today than it was in 1937, when very few people were imprisoned. This increase in prison numbers has occurred in the face of a lenient criminal justice system that, except in serious cases, will only send convicted criminals to jail after all other methods of punishment have been tried and failed. One consequence of this reduction in the frequency with which convicted criminals are imprisoned, which also accounts for the increased size of the prison population, is the increased proportion of those in jail who are serving longer sentences for more heinous crimes. In 1937, only 800 male prisoners were serving sentences of over three years, a mere nine per cent of the total. By 1997, 23,000 were, making up more than half the prison population.[1] Under these circumstances, to call, as the Lord Chief Justice has done, for a halving of the prison population is inane. Rather, we should accept that the prison population ought to be doubled, not because larger numbers of individuals should be sent to jail, but because those serious criminals for whom prison is now increasingly reserved should be made to serve even longer sentences.

However, there are two quite different reasons why many prison sentences should be lengthened which, in general, reinforce one another, but which can be seen to conflict when looked at in detail. One is retributive and the other is utilitarian. The retributive reason can best be explained by looking at the contrasting case of those criminals convicted of relatively petty offences who have been sent to jail for six months. On any fair scale of *proportionality*, serious criminals ought to be made to serve sentences at least 20 times as long as these relatively petty offenders. And they should be serving such terms even after receipt of remission. If, as a result of the meddling of the European Court of Human Rights, it becomes forbidden for remission to be granted for good behaviour in prison, then there should be no remission at all. If, in the course of carrying out other criminal acts, criminals commit murder either as means to their perpetration or to avoid these very long sentences, then they should have to serve life without parole.

The Lord Chief Justice's scheme for allowing the least wicked murderers to serve much shorter minimum sentences than they are presently made to do is a very reasonable one. However, it carries the corollary that more heinous murderers should, upon conviction, have to remain in prison until they die. The average length of time served might well remain the same, but there would be a greater spread of times served that would reflect the very real differences in degrees of desert as between one murderer and another.

Yet, the amount of time for which any given criminal deserves imprisonment for his or her crime can only be decided by making complex decisions about the appropriate level of retribution for each particular individual crime. As was argued by that great British upholder of retributive justice, the Victorian judge James Fitzjames Stephen,[2] you cannot decide in advance what the sentence, even the minimum sentence, should be for a particular category of crime. A domestic burglar whose crime consists in breaking into a garden-shed during the day and stealing a mower hardly deserves to go to jail, even on the basis of three strikes and out. By contrast, a gang of domestic burglars who break into a house at night, terrify and threaten the householders, trash their belongings, and make off with personal items as well as valuables, would, in a just and proportional world, have to serve prison terms of the order of ten years. This would deserve such sentences because of the utter contempt with which they have treated ordinary respectable citizens living out their everyday lives. Yet each of these two offences falls into general category of domestic burglary.

From a retributive point of view, what is outrageous is not that deciding the appropriate sentence for an offence is complex, for that is inevitable. It is, rather, the unwillingness of the liberal élite to concede that the most serious crimes deserve correspondingly severe punishments. These crimes are deliberately carried out by sane, autonomous individuals who have chosen to perform them in full knowledge of the public's abhorrence of them and of the consequences they have for their victims. It is at this point that justice is simple. The social origins of those who perpetrate them is irrelevant. They are free agents who could have chosen otherwise, even if this meant their choosing lesser forms of deviance. It is wrong to choose to be a criminal, but it is still far, far worse to choose to commit the most serious of criminal acts that involve the deliberate, indeed, the malicious and gratuitous infliction of harm on others. Why could not their perpetrators have stuck to benefit fraud or petty theft from big organisations? That they chose not to, but instead sought out as their victims individuals whom they terrorised or injured is what defines those who commit the more heinous crimes as 'Outlaws'. Breaking the law is not the point—many ordinary citizens do break the law. What sets Outlaws apart is the contempt they show for their victims.

There is, however, a second reason why longer sentences are needed in the case of those crimes that impinge the most on ordinary citizens. This reason is the need to protect the public. While criminals are locked up, they remain incapacitated to an extent not possible when subject to 'community sentences'. They can no longer commit crimes, except against fellow prisoners, and, in the case of these crimes, those who commit them should still be made to suffer severe penalties. Prisoners deserve protection from criminals like everyone else; the vulnerable should be segregated and their assailants placed in solitary confinement. However, for the time, and preferably a longer time, during which Outlaws are incarcerated, citizens are spared the risk of further depredations at their hands.

From this point of view, however, it is obviously more useful to lock up the more efficient criminals. It is easy to argue the case for locking up for a long period a serial robber or serial rapist. The more interesting case is that of domestic burglars or the snatch thief proto-mugger whose criminal activities cause considerable distress to their victims. It makes sense to impose longer sentences upon the more productive members of these groups, especially the younger ones. More crime is prevented by locking a man up who commits two hundred burglaries a year than one who only manages fifty. A 22-year-old burglar has a long career in front of him; a 40-year-old burglar may well be on the verge of giving up. By extension, a drug habit is not so much a mitigating circumstance but a reason for imposing a longer sentence upon anyone with one who is convicted for burglary, since if they are inclined towards burglary anyway, their addiction means they are likely to commit more of them. Yet none of these considerations has anything to do with retribution or desert. The young, strong, drug-taking, productive burglar is no worse morally speaking than a tired, ageing, 'time-I-gave-this-lark-up', it's-a-young-man's-game', less frequently active burglar, whose rate of offending has been slowed down by beer swilling induced obesity. Yet the case for the lengthier preventive detention of the former is a strong and rational one.

There is even a case for treating more severely those criminals who come from the least privileged backgrounds. The case is not that they are more deserving of punishment, but that, other things being equal, they are more likely to re-offend. Here, we are no longer talking of the moral responsibility each individual has for their actions which, except in obvious cases of diminished responsibility, can be neither shirked nor ignored. Rather, we are talking a more tough-minded version of the language of aggregates and probabilities belonging to those who perceive individuals and their acts in terms of cause and effect.[3] In practice, there is no simple way out of having to use both modes of argument. Each individual is an autonomous responsible agent who should always be treated as such. Yet we can also make predictions about how people will behave and we should act on this basis.

Retribution, innocence and rights

Charles Murray is strikingly accurate when he divides Britain's population into two antagonistic groups—the 'Citizens' and the 'Outlaws'. Those who belong to the latter group are those serious offenders who habitually prey on members of the former group. Clearly, as Murray says, 'the law should favour the Citizens'. Yet, from the account he gives, it appears members of Britain's liberal criminal justice élite do not see it that way. If Murray is right, they too are enemies of the people, albeit in a very different sense.

The problem with Britain's criminal justice élite is their insistence on conducting the argument about how criminals should be treated in terms of the criminal's putative 'rights': 'rights' when accused and tried, 'rights' when imprisoned, and 'rights' upon release. They justify their imputation to criminals of these supposed 'rights' by reference to abstract principles and traditional practice, or else with one eye kept on the interfering, uncomprehending, distant busybodies in the European Court of Human Rights.

None of them ever seems to ask how much any of these supposed ' rights' of the criminal costs society, or how severe would be the consequences for criminals of doing away with any of these supposed rights. Here, again, in face of this absolutist nonsense on stilts, there is room for a utilitarian, piece-meal and marginalist approach. An economist or a Benthamite might well ask what the costs and benefits are of the marginal item of 'rights', and he would be justified in doing so. No-one, not even a New Labour Home Secretary, is proposing to abolish all rights of criminals or suspected criminals. Total abolition of their rights might work in the same way as the criminal justice system 'worked' in Eastern Europe under socialism. It was safe to walk through the streets of Leningrad at night (you cannot say that of St Petersburg), or leave your car with impunity in the streets of Karl Marx Stadt (you cannot do so in Chemnitz) . There was little chance of escape in the lands of the Soviets and the Stasi where punishment could be very severe. Criminals lacked rights because no one enjoyed any. It is precisely to avoid living in a society of this kind that we have entrenched rights. No one is disputing that. It is the trade-off at the margin about which we are arguing, not the very nature of the society in which we live.

It is absurd to suppose Outlaws should enjoy exactly the same rights as Citizens do. Obviously, members of both groups share some rights in common which should not be abrogated. Criminals may not be treated as if they were traitors in wartime; and, even in wartime, traitors ought to be regarded as having some rights. That is not the point.

The very fact of being convicted of a serious offence—or, in some cases, of a series of minor offences—does warrant a forfeiture of some rights. The convicted offender may rightly be locked up or deprived of a driving licence or passport. They are then no longer free or at least have lost the right to drive or travel abroad . In an era of high crime, why should not those found guilty of serious crime have their rights subsequently curbed, although certainly not reduced to zero, even after serving their full terms of imprisonment in order better to enable the authorities to obtain subsequent convictions more quickly and with greater certainty and frequency?

Those who oppose heavy penalties for serious crime are always telling us that what deters people from committing crime is the certainty of being caught, not the size of penalty they will suffer if caught. (Deterrence clearly results from the simultaneous effect of both factors combined, but let that pass.) However, if what these opponents of heavy penalties say is true, why do they also oppose reforms of the criminal justice system that would increase the number and certainty of convictions?

The only possible objection, and it is a very serious one, against curbing the rights of previously convicted criminals, subsequent to their having served their full terms of

43

imprisonment, is the risk that it might increase the number
of convictions of innocent persons.[4] This objection apart, it
is difficult to see why those with *serious* criminal records
should not, when accused, be afforded less by way of legal
protection from the authorities than the respectable should
be allowed to enjoy. Why should there be equal justice? If
the purpose of the rules of evidence is to prevent miscarriages of justice, then they are justified *for retributive
reasons—it is wrong to punish the innocent.* If, however, the
reason the rules are there is to protect ordinary citizens
from intrusion and hassle, it is difficult to see why those
who have serious criminal records should not be thought to
have forfeited any right to the same degree of protection,
even if those criminal records were acquired when they
were juveniles.

Part of the penalty for being convicted of a serious crime,
or even of a very large number of petty crimes, ought to be
that the convicted criminal acquires the status of being an
'Outlaw'. This would be a new legal category that would
carry with it liability to be treated by those who administer
the criminal justice system more arbitrarily than law-
abiding Citizens are allowed to be. In their dealings with
Outlaws, the police and prison authorities would not be
bound by those procedural constraints they would be
obliged to observe in their dealings with Citizens. Suffering
such loss of rights should be a corollary of acquiring the
status of an 'Outlaw' in Charles Murray's sense of the term.
In the interest of other people's safety, someone deemed to
be one should become subject to forms of social control from
which 'Citizens' should be exempt. Being an 'Outlaw' carries
with it a negative legal status.

To determine anyone's guilt or innocence in the first
place, however, is not a simple matter. It can go wrong. The
changes that Charles Murray proposes to the rules concern-
ing the admissibility of evidence are far more problematic
than he supposes, and precisely because of the retributive
framework he has created. A utilitarian system of criminal
justice[5] can tolerate a number of mistaken convictions and
cases of false imprisonment in order to secure conviction of

a larger number of the truly guilty, but a retributive system of justice cannot.

One of the central principles of a retributive system of criminal justice is that the innocent should not be made to undergo punishment. In a non-retributive system of justice, no questions are asked about moral blame and penalties are imposed merely to enforce general compliance with rules, almost as a form of strict liability. Here, it does not matter too much if a few people are wrongly penalised. No doubt, the innocent will be angry at having to pay a fine, and may even choose to go to jail rather than pay, but no one is saying that they *deserve* to be punished.

Acquiring a serious criminal conviction is another matter, since it usually implies the convicted person has been found guilty of having deliberately and unambiguously inflicted harm on another in a way citizens regard as morally wrong. For this reason, rather than simply because the penalties are heavier, it is important in criminal cases that society takes pains to avoid convicting anyone who is innocent. It may well be that disclosing the past record of an innocent defendant would not increase the likelihood of their being falsely convicted. It is just one more piece of evidence to be assessed like any other, and probably one that is less difficult for a jury to weigh up than technical forensic evidence or arguments about a company's accounts or even the accuracy of eyewitness identification.[6] Whether disclosure of previous convictions would increase the rate of mistaken convictions is an empirical question; it is not an inalienable right that they never should be disclosed.

It is difficult to see, though, how it would be possible to allow past accusations that were never proceeded with to be brought up at the trial of anyone without significantly increasing the risk of securing mistaken convictions. How could a jury assess any such 'evidence'? It would be particularly difficult for a jury to do so in cases of alleged date-rape, if those who levelled the earlier accusations could not be cross-examined. To bring up as evidence such accusations without defendants being able to cross-examine those making them *would* be a denial of their rights.

A conviction is a fact, but an accusation has to be disputable in open court. It is for this reason that it is particularly dishonest of governments, with the agreement and connivance of the criminal justice élite, to manipulate the rules of evidence in sex cases merely to increase the rate of successful convictions. Such manipulations may well result in more convictions, but it needs to be openly accepted that they will almost certainly result in increased numbers of convictions of the innocent. On the basis of such evidence as we have, the likelihood of erroneous convictions in sex cases seems greater than in other kinds of case.[7] This is because of the trickiness of the evidence, depending as it does on one person's word against another and on subjective perceptions at the time that are inevitably distorted by memory.

In the United States, the striking increase in the number of mistaken convictions for rape since the early 1970s is probably due to the increased pressure to which the authorities there have been subject to obtain convictions for rape.[8] From this point of view, although it is easy to see why it was chosen, date-rape was just about the worst example, as a retributivist, Murray could have selected. My point, though, has a wider validity. For example, such are the dangers of using eye-witness identifications as evidence that there may well be a case for stronger legal safeguards than at present in connection with their use, even if their introduction made it harder for convictions to be secured,[9] and took us further away still from simple justice.

Outlaws, Citizens and the Liberal Élite

From Charles Murray's essay, there emerges a new picture, or at least a new dimension, of how British society is stratified. At the top of the pyramid of power stands a small progressive élite, of which the criminal justice élite forms but one section. Their values and priorities differ radically from those belonging to the group below them, 'the Citizens', a group whom the élite can ignore and disdain with impunity. The relationship between these two groups is one of conflict. On the basis of Murray's data, it seems that there has ceased to be any community of interest or outlook between them.

At the bottom of the system come 'the Outlaws'. This group is set apart from the Citizens by their willingness either to commit serious crimes against others or persistently to molest them to the point where the cumulative consequences are serious. This last class grew markedly in size and predatory boldness during the last half of the twentieth century. The relationship between the Citizens and Outlaws is again one of conflict, the former being victims of the latter. The conflict between Citizens and the criminal justice élite has arisen and intensified because of the failure of this small and powerful group to protect the Citizens from the Outlaws while increasingly denying Citizens the possibility of defending themselves. This conflict is not, nor should it be regarded as being, about the law or rights or abstract justice; it is about power.

There exists an implicit contract between the people and the state whereby the people grant to the state a monopoly over the use of legitimate force in return for protection and safety. In the last half of the nineteenth and first half of the twentieth century, it seemed to be a good bargain. The incidence of crime fell and then remained low, the streets were safe and homes were secure.[10] Following this period of success, the criminal justice élite became progressively more liberal in outlook while the Citizens continued to feel their interests were being protected by the élite, a group whom citizens perceived as being an extension of themselves and one that shared their perception of Citizens as virtuous and Outlaws as wicked.

It is no longer like that. The Outlaws can act with impunity, safe in the knowledge that the risk of being apprehended and punished is very low. If Citizens retaliate, the state can and will treat them with great severity, either by using the criminal law or by providing legal aid to aggrieved Outlaws. Citizens are vulnerable because they have jobs, an income, homes and possessions. This means they can easily be located, identified, and proceeded against, and also that they have something to lose. If a burglar assaults a householder, he will probably then escape and never be found. Even if subsequently caught in mid-career, the chances are small of his being convicted of the original assault. If the householder were to sue a burglar, or come to that a mugger for injuries received, it would be pointless. The householder would not get legal aid and the person sued has no accessible assets: the proceeds of crime are invisible, hidden, untaxed and usually spent very quickly. By contrast, a householder who injures a burglar cannot escape and is liable to be prosecuted by an obsessive Crown Prosecution Service determined to preserve the state's monopoly of violence. If, in addition, the injured burglar decides to proceed with a civil action against the householder with the assistance of legal aid, the latter may be ruined. The dice are loaded in favour of the wicked. Furthermore, burglars tend to be young, male, strong and risk takers who often work in pairs or a group so that the householder needs an equalizer. Yet it is only burglars who have access to firearms. Britain is a country with such strict gun controls that the ordinary citizen cannot acquire one. Where would he or she buy one? Who would grant them a licence? If, by chance, they kept an 'illegal weapon' at home, the penalties for being found doing so are severe; unlike criminals, respectable citizens cannot afford a conviction of this kind. By contrast, there is a rising level of crimes involving the use of guns in Britain committed by Outlaws. Since 1964, the murder rate in Britain has doubled, but the number of female victims, that is, domestic murders, has remained constant.[11]

The same point may be made in relation to hooliganism in general. The police are unable to prevent it and the perpetrators feel secure. Yet, if the citizens were 'to take the law into their own hands' and run the delinquent families out of town, there would be hysterical denunciations of them as vigilantes and lynch mobs, and severe penalties would be imposed. *Very late in the day*, the government has introduced Anti-Social Behaviour Orders but only in order to be seen to be doing something. They are frequently breached and nothing happens. They will probably become just another way to avoid locking Outlaws up. Even so, they have already been challenged in the courts, out of legal aid

paid for by the Citizens, by those who have been subject to
them who claim them to have infringed their rights. These
challenges have so far failed but there is no end to the
fanaticism of human rights lawyers armed with due process
and equal rights. They will find a wormhole and turn it into
a loophole.

The Citizen today is hemmed in by the government,
thoroughly regulated and controlled, and the subject of
arbitrary intrusion and inquiry, particularly where the
raising of revenue by the state is concerned. VAT inspectors
have more power than the police.[12] The Outlaw escapes all
this. He lives in a world of cash transactions of which many
involve the proceeds of illegal activities, of the wilful
disregarding of planning controls that he knows will never
be enforced due to the law's delay and the insolence of state-
funded human rights lawyers. He regularly drives without
a licence, insurance or MOT certificate, and rarely pays
fines, child support, or rent arrears. In modern Britain, only
the Outlaw is free. The only constraint that can be imposed
on him is prison and the criminal justice élite is reluctant
to use it. Imagine the frustration of ordinary Citizens whose
lives are ones of endless regulation when they see the
wicked escape all this. It is worst for the honest and decent
poor whose lives are a perpetual struggle to make ends
meet. They are subject to economic loss and physical insult
from those who don't even care where the ends are. They
are crushed from both sides and their voice is only to be
heard in the tabloid newspapers.

It is clear that this situation must be reversed. The way
to do so is to make 'Outlaw' into a legal status that is
earned by an accumulation of points awarded for anti-social
behaviour, even as a juvenile, but with the greatest number
of points being awarded for serious crimes. Just as a driver
who has accumulated enough points for speeding or careless
driving may lose his or her licence or suffer instant disquali-
fication for doing something downright dangerous, so, too,
cumulative or dangerous criminality would mean Outlawry.
For someone to acquire Outlaw status would mean a
diminution, though not an extinction, of their legal rights in

both civil and criminal contexts. If, in the course of a crime or even a dispute, an Outlaw should injure a Citizen, he or she should be punished with exemplary severity. Violence on the part of an Outlaw, even under provocation, should be regarded as worse than that committed by a Citizen. Obviously a Citizen should be allowed to use sufficient force when necessary to repel or detain a burglar, rapist, or robber without being subject to criminal penalty or civil action and regardless of the status of the wrong-doer. But where what happened or what degree of force was necessary to repel or detain an assailant is in dispute, then the Outlaw status of the assailant would carry decisive weight in deciding the matter.

Likewise an Outlaw would be under a far greater degree of surveillance, regulation, and data-recording than a Citizen. Outlaws would be treated the way serious sex-offenders are today. It is stupid, wrong, and pointless to force ID cards on a reluctant British population who have never previously had to carry them except in war-time, but Outlaws, and only Outlaws, should be compelled to carry them at all times. They could also be smart cards providing instant access both to a certain confirmation of a person's identity and to their past history. The threat of the creeping surveillance state would be averted by insisting that Citizens be exempt from these constraints and, indeed, the separating out of Outlaws in this way could be used as an opportunity for freeing up the Citizens. A structured inequality would thus be created. For most Outlaws, their having this status would not be permanent, since age dampens enthusiasm for an unquiet life. It would be possible to add to the list further legal and welfare disad-vantages to the point where it would be a category to be avoided and from which to seek escape by the only method possible: a long period of exemplary conduct. Giving priority to controlling the Outlaws would give a meaning and focus to police paperwork and computerised records, much of the rest of which could be safely abandoned.

The status of someone being an Outlaw would affect police behaviour. Rounding up the usual suspects at present tends to provoke the complaints of 'It's not fair, they're always picking on me' and 'Whenever anything happens they come round looking for me'. Assigning Outlaw status to serious and persistent offenders would place their rounding up as suspects upon a formal and legitimate basis. Many of the constraints that currently hamper the police in relation to search and seizure would be suspended in the case of Outlaws. Having this status would also have a very strong influence on the severity of sentences to which someone would be liable upon further conviction, particularly in the case of younger criminals: not as retribution, but as preventive detention. The jail population would rise substantially and this would require the necessary prior investment in plant and provision for running costs, well in advance of its introduction. It is doubtful though whether it would be wise for a person's status as Outlaw to be disclosed to magistrates or a jury before they make any decision as to the guilt or innocence of anyone. Its very power might bias the verdict.

Such a measure would restore the proper balance of power between Citizen and Outlaw. It would be an emphatically anti-Rawlsian measure, a decisive refutation of the philosophy and policy of the progressive élite, a formal recognition and exploitation of the power of exclusion.

Such a measure could be enacted only if the powers usurped by the criminal justice élite were restored to the people, whether by re-emphasising parliamentary sovereignty and making crime a bitterly contested electoral issue or by deciding such questions by referenda. The criminal justice élite would remain insulated when involved in making decisions about particular cases, but they would lose their autonomy in policy-making. We need rule by Citizens, not lawyers.

It is also time to realize that the Home Office has long been a force for bad, a potential saboteur of the Home Secretary—one Home Secretary has said as much, a Sir Humphrey with horns, an enemy of the people. Just look at the difference between its literature and that of the Department of Health. The latter department is activist and 'healthist' in the manner of Marc Lalonde,[13] endlessly exploiting small correlations to frighten people about every aspect of their daily lives. The Home Office goes out of its way to minimise the appearance of high levels of crime and its impact, unless, of course, it is a politically correct cause in which case they are played up. In the early 1980s, responses to the British Crime Survey suggested there were about 1,800,000 violent crimes against persons over the age of 16 in any one year, many of which were not reported to the police. However, readers of the official report were carefully told that in only 12 per cent of cases did victims of them need any sort of medical attention and that in less than one per cent of cases were the victims admitted to hospital.[14] Why were the statistics presented in this way? Why were we not told that 216,000 individuals who had been attacked needed and sought medical attention and that many thousands of victims of violent crime had been admitted to hospital? Imagine how differently the figures would have been presented by a government department seeking more restrictive safety legislation. We would have been tabloided into anxiety. If you would like to know what is happening to violent crime in Britain today, talk to a hospital dentist; they have the job of patching up the increasing number of facial injuries. No wonder you can't find an NHS dentist. They are all busy on fight victims. One of the criminologists at the University of Wales who is fearful lest the truth gets out about rising levels of violence no longer talks to the Professor of Dentistry!

As Charles Murray pointed out, in the 1980s the Home Office would use every excuse it could to evade the implications of the rise in reported crime. It said it was all due to increases in reporting and improvements in recording and to the reclassification of offences that made them appear more serious. Those compiling the statistics, on the whole, do so honestly, although I do know of one case in which an attempt to classify those convicted according to their level of 'dangerousness' was deliberately sabotaged by a researcher who feared such knowledge would be used in a punitive way.

The fear of punitiveness is the entire key to Home Office thinking. I can remember, at the beginning of the 1990s, being placed in a confrontation on television with a Home Office official on the question whether levels of crime were rising. I said that you could not say very much on the basis of a single year's figures but that over a 35-year period there had been a massive rise. The woman from the Home Office replied, 'We mustn't be punitive, must we?' No mention had been made of punishment by me or the chairman. I had in fact been thinking of quite other matters to do with the elephantiasis of the welfare state and the decline of religion. But, for her, the factual question of whether or not there had been a rise in crime was determined by what the public's response to the news of such a rise might be.

In other areas, the Home Office technique for fending off accountability and transparency is simply to conceal the data. It deliberately withholds from free access even quite old material in the Public Record Office, and, in the future, will quickly find ways of not complying with any Freedom of Information Act. Whether or not you obtain access will depend on whether you are likely to make deductions from the data that fit the prejudices of the Home Office.

When studies carried out by the Home Office *are* released, the amount of publicity they are given and the degree to which they are regarded as accurate is determined by policy. The Home Office uses a method I have named 'one-eyed rigour' (this term is copyright Christie Davies). If the results are an embarrassment for it, then a hunt is made for small flaws in the design or execution of the research that will invalidate the findings. If the results are to its liking, then no such hunt is undertaken. Let me give an example. The Home Office did an excellent study on a topic that is a real as well as a politically correct problem— racial attacks on Asian shopkeepers. I did not know that this work was in progress and had independently written to the Home Office suggesting such a study be done. I was then summoned to the Home Office to see the results. The study revealed that a disproportionately high number of these racial incidents had been perpetrated by West Indians. The researcher, a very decent young chap, literally became frightened of me when I pointed this out and was amazed and relieved when I complimented him on his courage and honesty. At this point, a senior female administrator intervened, claiming there were problems in the sampling and that the results should not be taken seriously. There were, indeed, a few problems with the research, but they did not in any way disturb the robustness of its findings. Should there ever emerge the data recently collected by the Home Office on how many crimes prisoners in jail admit to having committed in the year before being locked up, we may be sure it will be hedged around with irrelevant qualifiers, intended in all senses to minimize the findings.

The Home Office's moment of triumph, and this is very relevant to Charles Murray's thesis, was the enactment of the Criminal Justice Act of 1991 which became known as the criminal's charter.[15] Its aim was to eliminate the possibility of persistent property offenders ever being sent to jail. Magistrates were told that, when deciding whether to lock an offender up, they should only consider the most serious of a long string of offences, plus one other, that is, two in total. They were forbidden to look at all of them in aggregate or conclude that here was a cynical and persistent thief who had calculated the odds of being caught and set these against the profits of the trade. In addition they could not take previous convictions into account. It meant the end of custodial sentences and even of hefty fines, for fines were fixed not in £s but in 'units'. The fine to be paid was then calculated by multiplying this figure by the offender's disposable income. Thieves did not have to pay heavy fines, for the same reason they do not pay tax—there is no mechanism by which to determine their income. Fences were delighted by the Act, for it meant those whom they employed as thieves no longer could be induced to grass them up to avoid a prison sentence. The network of crooked thieves who steal to order became safe and secure from interference by the police.

Many magistrates resigned rather than work with this crackpot scheme but it collapsed for a different reason. Citizens with an otherwise blameless record, and who, in general, were industrious, productive, and thrifty, were being fined very large sums for essentially trivial single offences or one-off cases of giving way to temptation. The then Home Secretary, a man of straw and putty, was replaced and the scheme dropped. However, what is remarkable is that such a stupid, unjust and unworkable scheme should ever have been designed and foisted on him by the bureaucrats of the Home Office.

As far as I know, none of those responsible for this section of the 1991 Act were ever sacked, demoted, or transferred to the Falkland Islands. The Home Office is still there with an unchanged ethos. A general who loses a battle can be sacked or sent to Limoges, a businessman can go bankrupt, a professional man become feeless, an academic made redundant when a department's research rating falls, but, in the Home Office, nothing succeeds like failure. It is time for the organisation to be split up into its component parts and those who work within that section dealing with crime be asked very firmly, 'Whose side are you on?' Citizens and Outlaws are on opposite sides and it is necessary that those in charge of criminal justice policy exhibit a very strong bias towards the Citizens. They must be firmly told that their duty is to protect the Citizens. They are not in the business of pursuing social justice or inclusion. Justice means protecting the innocent, rewarding the virtuous, and penalising the guilty. Justice is simple justice. Putting the word 'social' in front of it robs the term of all meaning. A social worker is not a worker, a social market economy is not a market economy, a social democrat is not a democrat, and social justice is not justice.[16]

The criminal justice élite should be viewed not as an aggregate of disinterested and detached individuals (which no doubt many of them are) but as a distinct group with common material and ideal interests. All senior bureaucrats want an expansion of their empires; it leads to a bigger pyramid with more room at the top, bigger salaries, faster promotion, and a greater exercise of central power. Human rights work and ambulance-chasing on behalf of criminals means fees for expensive lawyers, money far in excess of that paid to ordinary solicitors doing routine defence work on legal aid which does not pay at all well. The transfer of political power to judges means more judges and more powerful judges.

'Ideal interests' are a more complicated form of group self-interest. They involve being able to stamp a group's idea of how the world should be on other less influential sections of society, regardless of democratic accountability. We may well trust individual members of the criminal justice élite because we recognize them as men or women of integrity, but we have no reason to trust them as a class.

Rough Justice: Some Thoughts on Charles Murray's *Simple Justice*

John Cottingham

Charles Murray's hard-line essay offers a 'simple alternative' to what he sees as the flabby, soft-hearted 'progressive' attitude to criminal justice that (on his view) infects much of the legal establishment and others 'with high IQs and advanced degrees'. The simple alternative he calls 'retributive justice', and its 'primal function', he tells us, is to 'depersonalise revenge'. Invoking Immanuel Kant as his champion, Murray deploys the well-known Kantian thought -experiment, in which we are asked to imagine we are on an island and civil society is about to disband: should we first punish the last murderer remaining in prison? (Assume, for the sake of argument, we know he will not kill again.) If, with Kant, we say 'Yes: punishment must be imposed!', then, says Murray, we are 'retributivists at heart'.

But notice, to begin with, that revenge, even if 'depersonalised', is by its very nature radically distinct from retribution. Kant, to be sure, believed in retribution, but he was resolutely opposed to revenge. We cannot know what he would have said about the emotive example Murray opens with—the assault victim and her CS mace spray—but if her motive in spraying the chemical into the eyes of the assailant is 'Take *that*, and serve you right!', then the austere burgher of Köningsberg would have strongly disapproved: 'No one, except God, is authorised to inflict punishment and to avenge the wrongs sustained by them'.[1] For Kant, any element of malice (and desire for revenge, he observes, is the 'sweetest form of malice') directly contravenes that virtue of sympathy, and indeed of forgiveness, which every human being should cultivate.

56

So is Kant after all a friend of those lily-livered progressives who apparently infest today's British legal establishment? By no means. He is adamant that we should not 'meekly tolerate' wrongs, and that 'rigorous' means of retribution can often be appropriate. But retribution, for Kant, is part of *justice*: it must be properly authorised, proportionate, and wholly purged of malice and anger. That is why a gut response to Kant's desert island thought-experiment tells us very little. To call ourselves Kantian retributivists, we need to agree not just on whether the offender has 'got it coming', but on the rationale for that response.

A rationale which invokes the desire on our part to 'pay someone back' for what they have done is revenge-centred; a rationale that requires the offender to pay for what he has done is, or may be, authentically retributive. One crucial difference here has to do with who is supposed to be doing the 'paying'. 'I'll pay you back for that!' is about requital, anger, hitting back, and has very little to do with justice. By contrast, 'The criminal deserves to pay (by being punished)' is (or may be) the proper retributive judgment of society.

This important distinction tends to get blurred by Murray's use of emotive examples and crude dichotomies ('cop' versus 'progressive'), and his milking of the currently hot issue of whether burglary victims should be allowed to 'have a go'. But, despite all that, could one not apply a principle of charity and assume that what Murray is really interested in defending is proper judicially administered retribution (not individual retaliation or unlicensed revenge)? That may well be what he takes himself to be doing; but the implications of being a true retributivist are in fact far more complex than he seems prepared to recognise. Anyone who seriously buys into the idea of genuine (Kantian-style) retributive justice, will find themselves committed willy-nilly to a complex moral package, not every part of which, I suspect, may turn out to be quite so palatable to the 'cops' or hardliners as they had at first hoped.

Fiat justitia ruat caelum: Let justice prevail though the heavens fall. Kant, good retributivist that he was, subscribed to this maxim. For if justice goes, he said, there is no longer any value in human beings living on the earth.[2] But there are two aspects to justice's prevailing, a positive and a negative: justice must always be exacted; but, also, nothing must ever be done at the cost of injustice.

Take the first first. If it is just that offenders should be punished (and retributivists believe this), then we indeed have an obligation to punish them. If a wrong has been committed, we cannot just 'let it go'. That is the point of Kant's desert island example in the *Rechtslehre*. A murder or other serious crime upsets the moral order: simply to ignore it, or to disband and walk away, would be to allow the wrong to 'stand', or 'remain valid' (*gelten*) as Hegel later put it, developing the Kantian idea.[3] The obligation to punish arises not out of some kind of macho 'hardliner' stance, or platitudinous slogan about being 'tough on crime', but out of the deep intuition that a moral wrong calls for a *response*. Punishing belongs with a group of measured moral responses (the bestowal of blame is another example), the abandoning of which would not be a sign of enlightenment, but rather an indication that our system of civilised human values had started to unravel.

Given this reasoning behind Kant's insistence on the need to punish, then the Kantian framework turns out to be very different from Murray's. For a large part of Murray's argument invokes the idea of civil values having partially unravelled already: the burglar has 'stepped over a line and become an outlaw', and so (we are gleefully told) he has 'no complaint if the homeowner pulls out a shotgun and shoots him as he attempts to flee'. The concept of the 'outlaw' takes us a world away from Kant's measured retribution: it is borrowed from the frontier culture of the Wild West, where posters proclaimed that a dangerous man was 'Wanted, Dead or Alive'. The premise here was that of a largely lawless environment where there was often no means of bringing bullies to justice; and the 'dead or alive' slogan expressed precisely the thought that justice (apprehension, trial, sentence) was secondary to eliminating the (supposed) malefactor by any available means.

In such 'wild' circumstances, one might feel, there was no alternative: the end justified the means. But even if such utilitarian reasoning were to be regarded as acceptable in lawless or chaotic environments, it does not follow that it can be properly adopted for use in civil society. If one is going to follow the Kantian line on these matters, the end can never justify the means. Kant's desire that justice should prevail come what may (and here we come to the second, negative, aspect of his maxim) explicitly rejects the lure of any utilitarian means-ends reasoning about law enforcement: to believe in justice is not just to insist that justice be done, but to insist that unjust means are absolutely prohibited.

Criminal desert, according to Kantian principles, is sufficient for just punishment, but is also *necessary*. To be a Kantian, in this sense, about retributive justice is to set one's face against measures, however socially or politically expedient, which countenance likely injustice for the sake of some desired goal, such as a reduced overall crime rate—however laudable in itself that goal may be. Suppose, to take a classic example, we could secure better obedience to the law by framing an innocent man and subjecting him to widely publicised severe punishment: that would be absolutely prohibited according to Kantian principles of retributive justice. Murray, you may object, is not proposing anything like this. But in recent times hardliners have proposed a string of expediency measures which, in the name of securing better law enforcement, allow the possibility that an innocent person may more easily be convicted. Weakening of the right to silence, and erosion of the right to trial by jury—ancient rights now lost or on the way to being lost by British citizens—are two of the most shocking examples of this tendency. And Murray adds his voice to the clamour for a new erosion: allowing evidence of prior arrests. This is proposed under a banner that, again, *sounds* quite Kantian in its moralistic solemnity: the judicial process should be a 'solemn search for the truth'—and what could be more relevant to ascertaining the truth than the character of the accused? But unfortunately, as Murray develops his argument, truth turns out to be an early casualty: in the space of a few paragraphs, 'evidence of prior *arrests*' is subtly and slyly transmuted into 'data about prior *behaviour*', which then, a page or so later, becomes 'prior *criminal record*' (emphasis supplied). The ancient and central principle of British justice, that an accused is presumed innocent until proven guilty, has here been brusquely set aside— hardly a proceeding that shows much concern for justice. If the failure to distinguish being arrested from being guilty is deliberate, it is alarming; if inadvertent, then it hardly bodes well for the author's professed confidence in the ability of the 'good sense' of the average jury to make the necessary distinctions.

Behind the vaunted Kantianism, then, lurks something disturbing and profoundly unKantian: a hugely simplified form of retributivism that insists on Kant's positive thesis (that crime requires a punitive response), but effectively filters out the crucial negative corollary, that injustice cannot be countenanced. The 'retributive' policy advocated by Murray envisages 'doubling, probably tripling and perhaps quadrupling' the current prison population. But notice that this would be achieved, on Murray's plan, not by making judges tougher on convicted offenders (for Murray admits that they are almost as tough in exacting retribution as they were 50 years ago), but by eliminating the leniency that 'resides in the ways that bringing an accused to trial has been made so difficult and time-consuming'. So what this lamentable 'leniency' consists of, so far as one can see, is the network of procedural rights and safeguards designed to protect the innocent from being wrongfully brought to trial and wrongfully convicted.

The stark assumption at work here, and frequently stated quite explicitly in the paper, is that 'for practical purposes' there are two classes in society—the 'Citizens' and the 'Outlaws'. The state of being an outlaw, Murray argues with staggering insouciance, 'implies reduced rights during the judicial process'. But the whole point of the judicial process, one might have hoped, is to determine whether an individual falls into the class of offenders or not; so that a system of 'reduced rights' during the judicial process would turn out to be prejudicial in the most literal and terrifying sense: guilt is pre-judged. What appears to have happened here is that the concern to deal with the 'outlaws' has, in effect, trumped all other concerns— even the concern for a fair and impartial judicial process; indeed Murray explicitly states that when citizens are up against 'outlaws' the playing field should not be 'level'.

The problem here is not just an epistemological one—as if, were we somehow to know for certain who was a criminal and who was innocent, Murray's simplified form of retributivism would be acceptable. That the difficulties are merely evidential or epistemic is insinuated by Murray's fantasy of the 'truth serum' forcibly administered to accused persons (witnesses, strangely, are not mentioned), so that, in effect, we could know in advance who is an Outlaw and who a Citizen, and could then get on with exacting retribution. But justice, as Kant saw, is far more complex than this. It is about respect for persons, never using a human being as a means to an end, never employing measures that erode someone's human dignity, never countenancing a procedure or practice that makes an individual merely instrumental in the production of a social goal. The safeguards that Murray would overthrow are not merely evidential rules, designed to make sure that the facts to be considered by the courts are reliably ascertained (important though that is); they are intimately bound up with the fundamental rule of retributive justice: no punishment without guilt, justly and fairly established. If, merely by being caught up in the judicial process, I am to lose my right to be presumed innocent until proved guilty, then the basic idea of justice as fairness is flouted.

What is often forgotten about retribution is the moral vision that underlies it. Retributive punishment is administered not as a means to an end—to reduce future crime, to deter, to reform, rehabilitate, placate victims, satisfy the tabloid press—nor for any other reason whatsoever other than that it is, in each individual case, deserved. For us to judge that a fellow citizen merits punishment, a host of moral structures must be in place: the offender must be regarded as a moral agent, capable of rational choice, who freely and knowingly chose to break a just law. Almost every element of this framework involves complex rules and procedures that are intricate and costly to implement. Convictions, for example, would often be much easier to secure without the requirement of *mens rea*—the need for the prosecution to prove the requisite intent and/or knowledge; but that is the price that has to be paid if we are interested not merely in 'enforcement' or 'control', but in whether the offender deserves the penalty. But the attendant reduction in 'efficiency', or ease of conviction, is the price we pay for a system that is built not on expediency but on *justice*.

Calls to 'toughen' the system will always be with us. Home secretaries want more convictions; journalists (because it sells their papers) want more convictions; the police want more convictions (that is not their fault, but simply a function of how they measure success: convictions are to the police as publications are to academics). Judges often want convictions—as in the famous *Penn and Mead* case of 1670 when jurors who refused to convict two Quakers of unlawful assembly were sent to prison—a case which led, on appeal, to the enshrining of the principle of the 'sanctity of the jury room' (another ancient principle of justice, incidentally, that is currently being 'reviewed' under pressure from the hardliners).

The rules of justice are so easily seen as obstacles to the popular goal of increasing the conviction rate. But those who believe in retributive justice do not want convictions *simpliciter*: they want just and only just convictions. Murray bolsters his attack on the supposed leniency of the present system by citing his 'fury' when he served on a jury and found out afterwards about the accused's prior record. But if (as one assumes from the anecdote) he voted for acquittal, he must presumably have done so because, after carefully considering the evidence, he judged that the prosecution *had not proved its case*. What Murray is therefore calling for is a change in the system such that, in similar cases, *where the case has not been proved*, the jury will be able to convict on the basis of prior record. (And remember that Murray considers not only prior conviction, but even mere arrest, to be a legitimate part of the 'record' that should be disclosed.)

The Kantian moral vision is of a world where each individual human being is treated as an 'end in themselves', never as a means. Judicial rights and safeguards flow from that fundamental principle of 'respect for persons': you have a right to be judged fairly and equally, without coercion, without being forcibly medicated, by a jury of your peers, on your own merits, and on the evidence relevant to the case at hand. You have a right not to be judged in advance, not to be placed in the class of 'outlaws' merely in virtue of having been accused or arrested. None of these rights are ones you yourself would rationally be willing to forego, were your own reputation or livelihood to be in jeopardy. And given this (for no man is an island), fairness dictates that you do not deny to the least of your fellow citizens the self-same rights. *Fiat justitia!*

Nuanced Justice

Tom Sorell

I t is possible to be a retributivist without being a 'Cop' in Murray's sense, and without holding views about justice that are simple. Retributivism along these lines is preferable to Murray's. It is preferable because justice is not simple, and because the intuitions that make one a Cop are unstable. Or so I shall claim. A nuanced justice or a nuanced retributivism is not easy to argue for briefly, of course; but, since it can be reached by complicating a simple retributivism in clear ways, I hope that it will emerge in outline from what follows, and that it will seem plausible in the light of problems with Murray's own position.

I

The materials of Murray's argument are: (1) some hypotheticals; (2) an identification of two patterns of reaction to those hypotheticals; (3) a brief statement of theories of justice appropriate to each type of reaction; (4) an argument for one of those theories of justice; and (5) a statement of its implications for criminal law reform. I have some sympathy for stage (5) of Murray's argument, but much less for the rest. And I trace my disagreement to Murray's handling of the reactions to his hypotheticals.

There are seven hypotheticals, but two reflect cases that Murray consistently emphasises. These are cases of violent resistance or retaliation for assault or burglary. I quote the first hypothetical in full:

A woman is dragged into an alleyway by an unknown assailant. She sprays Mace into the assailant's eyes, enabling her to escape but causing permanent damage to the assailant's eyesight. Did the woman act rightly? Does the assailant have a just complaint against her?

64

*(1) The woman used disproportionate force, and the assail-
ant has a just complaint.*

*(2) Technically, the woman used disproportionate force, but
she should not be prosecuted and the assailant should
receive only nominal damages.*

*(3) The woman acted rightly and the assailant has no
complaint.*

Murray thinks (3) is the right answer, and also the
answer that would be given by a 'Cop', a person who is
consistently tough on crime. If his formulations (1) to (3) are
all there is to choose from, I would agree. But, as will
emerge, they are not.

Let us consider what there is to be said for (3). Perhaps
the most obvious thing is that acts in self-defence are
normally amply justified, whereas unprovoked assault
never is, or hardly ever is. Given that, how can the assailant
possibly complain? If he expected that the woman would be
too terrified to resist and was not prepared for Mace, that is
too bad. Using Mace against an assailant is not disproportionate as an act of self-defence, and Mace need not and
probably does not normally cause permanent damage. The
fact that it did cause permanent eye damage was not a
foreseeable consequence of what the woman did. In any
case, if the assailant did not expect his victim to defend
herself, if he expected meek submission, that only under-
lines the fact that he chose to assault someone he regarded
as harmless and defenceless, and attacking the harmless
and defenceless is worse than striking out against someone
who it seems can respond in kind. In short, the assailant is
claiming victimisation in a case where he has to be seen
either as predatory or as someone who initiated aggression,
not expecting aggression in return. In neither case can he
complain about the Mace or its effects.

That much, I think, can *reasonably* be said in favour of
reaction (3). But it is not impossible that someone would
want to go further, and claim that it is neither here nor
there whether self-defence in such a case is proportionate.
Suppose we alter the case in only this respect: instead of
Mace, a gun is used, and the attacker dies. Or consider a

more grisly variant still. The assailant badly misjudges his target, and drags into the alley a very capable torturer, who not only overpowers the assailant, but proceeds to inflict on him a very slow and painful death of the kind that a torturer specialises in. Let us stipulate that the torturer was not looking for trouble, but responded particularly vigorously to the assault. Is *this* victim of the assailant justified in what she does? The vigilante cinema genre perhaps softens us up to say that even in this case the assailant had it coming, much as if he had run up against the character of the tough cop Dirty Harry in a Clint Eastwood film. On this view, assailants deserve *whatever* they get.

Now I want to say that the intuitions that favour (3) in Murray's original case can also favour the more extreme, I think unreasonably extreme, verdicts in the variants of that case. This is what I meant by saying earlier on that the intuitions that make one a 'Cop' are unstable. Since it is at least arguable that no one ever deserves to be tortured to death, something has to be done to find a basis for (3) in the original case that does not end up permitting or justifying too much. The natural way of doing this is by saying that the actions of the victim of assault have to be directed at no more than self-defence. This condition outlaws enthusiastic vigilantes but permits Mace, even when it causes eye damage. And it properly raises questions about the lethal use of the gun. Was the gun being used in self-defence, or in revenge? Why wasn't its use only threatened? Was it the only thing available, or did the user of the gun think that the attacker had made her day by allowing her to use it on him? There are answers to the questions that justify the use of the gun. These answers do not, however, justify the conclusion that assailants deserve whatever they get.

Let us turn to a second hypothetical of Murray's. Here again a victim of crime does not simply bear the crime passively but reacts:

An offender enters a home to burgle it. Upon finding the owner at home, the offender flees into the street. The owner runs after the offender, catches him, and pummels him, causing bruises and contusions. Did the homeowner act rightly? Does the assailant have a just complaint against the homeowner?

(1)The homeowner was right in chasing the burglar out of the house, but wrong to pummel him, and the burglar has a just complaint.

(2)Technically, the homeowner should have just held the man for the police, but the homeowner should not be prosecuted and the burglar should receive only nominal damages.

(3)The homeowner acted rightly and the burglar has no complaint.

Here, too, the right answer, and the Cop's answer, is supposed to be (3). I think the correct answer is something different: namely:

(4) The homeowner was right in chasing the burglar out of the house, excusably pummelled him, and the burglar cannot reasonably complain.

Excusable actions are actions whose wrongness is counterbalanced or lessened by facts about the circumstances or the normal capacities and reactions of human beings. Pummelling people is normally wrong, and it is questionable in the hypothetical case under discussion as well. The reason is that, according to the description of the case, the burglar aborts his plan. When the homeowner acts, he is not obstructing the commission of the crime, but retaliating for the burglar's attempt to commit it. What the homeowner does has something to be said against it, namely, that violence that prevents no wrongdoing can be gratuitous. The retaliation is excusable, given the effect on a person of discovering an intruder in his home, but it is quite different from the action taken in the assault case, since that is necessary to frustrate the crime or to prevent a more serious one from being committed. The burglar, for his part, does not suffer permanent injury or injury disproportionate to the crime he planned to commit, and he could reasonably have foreseen such injury as a risk of entering an occupied house in order to burgle it. Once again, the effects on the criminal are different from those in the assault case.

Murray's and the Cop's reactions wrongly homogenise the two cases. As before, Murray sees both as cases where not to return answer (3) is to side unjustly with the criminal against the victim. I think we have in the two cases different kinds of injury to both victims and criminals, and my way of not returning answer (3) does *not* side with the criminal.

Not only are there possible answers to the second hypothetical that take the victim's side and that depart markedly from the Cop's answer; the suspicion must remain that in related cases the intuitions favouring the Cop's answer would push Cops in the direction of endorsing measures much more extreme than pummelling. Murray included Tony Martin, convicted of murder for killing a burglar, in the group on which he tested his hypotheticals, and Martin's case fits the description of the second of our pair of hypotheticals in several respects. The differences are that Martin's house was very isolated, making him particularly vulnerable to crime, that he had been burgled repeatedly, that he took special precautions against burglary, and that he shot dead one of a pair of youths who tried to burgle him. (The other was severely injured by Martin's dogs.) Unless one subscribes to the principle that burglars deserve everything they get, or that criminals deserve everything they get, death seems disproportionate as a response to burglary of the severity there was in the Martin case.

II

One of the attractions of retributivism, as well as being an attraction of the retributive element in legal systems that are a mix of retributivism and other things, is that retaliation is taken out of the hands of those directly concerned. This reflects the public or civic character of crime. The assailant in the first of the two hypotheticals and the burglar in the second are involved not only in injuring or harming another person. Their crimes also involve them in transactions with the rest of society. For each does something he knows is not only wrong but illegal and punishable by a public institution. The public institution is not a party to the assault or the burglary, and its punishment is not influenced directly by the technicolour experience of the man who finds the intruder or the woman who is dragged into the alley. Instead, the public institution has to disregard some of the technicolour and much of what makes each offence unique. It treats the dragging into the alley as one assault or attempted rape among others, and the illegal entry and attempted burglary as one among others. The classification of the crime as burglary or as attempted rape will carry a weighting for severity dictated not by anyone's sympathy for the victims, but by how the harm the crime involved measures up to other harms. Although the classification of crimes in law in general or for the purpose of getting a successful prosecution can seem to victims of crime to understate the harm done, or to leave some of the harm out of account altogether, the attempt to make offences comparable is important as a way of minimising injustice in the form of arbitrariness. Punishment should not reflect the shifting mood of the one in authority, or the uneven sympathies and outrages of the general public. It should reflect the harm done to the victim and the intentions of the offender, and it should reflect these using a single scale of harm and a consistent approach to intentions.

In English law, neither the assault nor the burglary that we have considered come into the category of the most serious crimes, and, as things stand in 2005, not even the most serious crimes recognised by the law, such as the repeated torture and murder of children, are legally punishable by death. This makes it a question what the courts are to do when killing has been the private citizen's retaliation for assault or burglary. I do not think that the answer to this question is simple, even if the assailants or burglars who are killed are repeat offenders. If the killings are condoned by the legal system, private citizens are

allowed to be their own judges of the severity of crime and
punishment, with all the arbitrariness and invitations to
excess that come with concentration on a single case, and a
case in which one is personally involved. On the other hand,
if the killings are treated as murders pure and simple, and
given life-sentences, as in the Martin case, then they are
wrongly lumped together with unprovoked crimes.

Murray thinks there *is* a simple answer in cases like the
Martin case, while also appearing to endorse the aspiration
to impersonal justice. He says that, unlike 'progressive
justice', retributive justice is not only 'simple in concept, it
is simple to implement' (p. 26). Although he does not spell
out the application of his hypothetical to the Martin case, it
is clear that he thinks that the people who attempted to
burgle Martin's house are what he calls 'Outlaws':

> The person who does kill, wound, rob, burgle or rape has stepped
> over the line and become an Outlaw. While he is in a state of
> Outlawry, he has lost many of the rights that Citizens enjoy.
>
> (p. 22).

In particular, the Outlaw's rights shrink to vanishing point
during the actual act of Outlawry. In a case like Martin's,
each burglar 'caused his own wounding or death' (p. 22). He
causes his own wounding or death by opting for Outlawry.
'Other retributivists,' Murray adds, 'take a less wide-open
view of the conditions under which lethal force is justified,
but the common principle is that criminals in the act of
committing a crime are taking their chances' (p. 22).

Now I think the line of thought just summarised confuses
private retaliation with retribution. If one asks whether
someone who is being raped or burgled can be expected to
act coolly and proportionately; if one asks whether someone
being raped or burgled can be blamed for lashing out in an
uncontrolled way, and perhaps in a way that was more
violent than was necessary to stop the rape or the burglary,
the answer seems to me to be a clear 'No'. But if one asks
whether a state institution can be criticised for punishing
burglary or rape with death, the answer is 'Yes'. This is
because retribution is not exacted in the course of a crime
by a victim who is in the grip of fear or rage, but by institu-

tions not personally involved which are acting according to rules that apply across a range of cases, once the facts and the application of the rules have in theory been coolly brought into balance. It is true that retribution has to give weight to the victim's experience and that, historically, it has not done so adequately under the justice systems of liberal democracy, but this does not imply that the standards of excusable retaliation are the same as standards of retributive justice. Nor does it make clear how retributive institutions are to deal with acts of excusable private retaliation or disproportionate private retaliation. It is one thing for each of *us* to sympathise with the rape or burglary victim who retaliates; it is another for a *court* to condone what they do; for that encourages or at least permits the substitution of private retaliation for public and impersonal retribution. And that is the end of systematic justice, and, maybe, of justice.

Murray gives the impression that he endorses a kind of impersonal justice when he outlines his vision of retributive justice:

> The primal function of a system of justice is to depersonalise revenge. The agreement, perhaps the most ancient of all agreements that make it possible for communities to exist, is that the individual will take his complaint to the community. In return, the community will exact the appropriate retribution—partly on behalf of the wronged individual, but also to express the community's moral values (pp. 18-19).

However, it quickly emerges that the 'community' is not represented by impersonal institutions that try to deal consistently with crime, treating everyone who comes before them the same. Instead, the community is supposed to show solidarity with its good members and revulsion at its bad ones. Its judgements are supposed to be informed by the records of its members (p. 19). People who never cross the line between citizenship and predation are supposed to have their 'supremacy' upheld over the claims of the outlaws.

Not only does this form of retribution seem to veer too close to condoning pre-emptive vigilante-ism, or ungoverned retaliation by citizens against outlaws; it draws the line between Outlawry and Citizenship in a way that seems arbitrary. Recall that an Outlaw in Murray's sense is anyone who commits an 'elemental predatory act': killing, wounding, robbing, burglary, or rape. Does not this category of 'elemental predatory act' amount to a rather mixed bag of offences? When it comes to the Outlaw not being able to expect any restraint from a victim, the most plausible case is that of an unprovoked life-threatening attack, and perhaps sexual crime. Non-violent property crimes seem not to rise to the relevant threshold, even when described as instances of elemental predation. In any case, killing, wounding and rape are surely worse than burglary. And there are burglaries and burglaries. If someone enters my garden in London at night and digs up and takes away a plant (something that has actually happened), is it excusable to retaliate as violently as one likes? What about having something taken by a burglar that one was about to deposit into a rubbish bin? Differently, what happens when the victim of Outlawry is himself or herself someone with a record of Outlawry? Are we to say, in that case, that burglary and rape don't count or aren't as urgently in need of being prosecuted as cases where a citizen is burgled or raped? What happens when a burglary or a robbery, say, in the form of shop-lifting of a low-priced item, is a first or second offence of someone who for decades has been a Citizen? These questions are supposed to indicate that the operation of retribution, as Murray understands it, may not be simple at all.

Some offences that do not fit the description of 'elemental predatory act', such as repeated verbal abuse and vandalism of public property, might seem to fall on the Outlaw side of an Outlaw/Citizen distinction. Yet no one thinks that people who engage in these offences forfeit all their rights. This is because a tenable Citizen/Outlaw distinction is probably closer to the distinction between non-aggressive, non-destructive behaviour and behaviour that is violent or destructive. When the distinction is drawn like this, however, it is only violent retaliation for extremely life-threatening or sexually violating outlawry, not violent retaliation for outlawry of all kinds, that the courts can even in principle be asked to condone. The Tony Martin case and the second hypothetical are then not necessarily able to be handled as Murray would like them to be.

III

I said at the beginning that I had more sympathy for some of the legal reforms Murray says simple justice requires than for simple justice itself. Let me enlarge on this sympathy, while continuing to distinguish my kind of retributivism from Murray's.

My kind of retributivism[1] punishes offences rather than characters, and it punishes serious offences severely. Indeed, its central tenet is that seriousness of punishment should be proportional to seriousness of crime, where seriousness is first and foremost a matter of harm to persons. It does not rule out in principle more severe punishments for serious crimes than currently are allowed by English law, but it acknowledges the dangers of irreversible and uncompensatable miscarriages of justice where the most serious crimes are punishable by death.

In retributivism, the lenience of a punishment for a serious crime is as much a departure from justice as the severity of a punishment for a minor crime. In non-retributive forms of justice, on the other hand, lenience is not a defect but a resource: it can be used as an incentive for reform, or as a way of deferring to the fact that a certain offence is out of character. The fact that this supposed resource is open to selective and partial use, however, is a great argument against employing it. For retributivists, penal laws make a binding promise to those convicted of crimes—the same promise as they make to every criminal. The form of the promise is that, if convicted, criminals will suffer for their crimes in the way that the law prescribes, in accordance with the seriousness of their crime, rather than in a way personal judgement or community judgement at a given time prescribes. In Kantian theories, to which I am attracted, the severity of punishment cannot be out of keeping with the humanity of the criminal, nor may the law be such as could not in principle be endorsed by all those subject to it. So, the humiliation of criminals is ruled out, as is their use as things, for example, as organ banks or experimental subjects. What such theories do not rule out as punishment is the infliction of the proportionate pain or captivity threatened by the relevant penal legislation. As my sort of retributivist sees things, someone who is guilty of a crime has repudiated or violated a law from which he can't rationally exempt himself. If the law, punishments and all, looks reasonable before he violates it, it should also look reasonable afterwards, when he has to suffer the punishment. It can't simply look reasonable so long as one does not feel its force. Citizenship means being subject to the law, including the punishments the law prescribes, and there can be a reason for endorsing the law even when one has broken it and has to suffer the consequences. There is a reason even if one's suffering the penalty makes no one else refrain from crime, even if the state is on the point of dissolution, even if the guilty person would not commit the crime again. The reason is the injury caused by different crimes, and the wrongness of being free to inflict such injury. The reason is not to do with the consequences of inflicting punishment or the circumstances of punishment.

Retributivism is a theory of punishment but not a theory of trial procedure. Yet clearly retributivism is a theory of the punishment of the guilty, and criminal trial procedure is a procedure for identifying the guilty and protecting the innocent from conviction. Retributivism takes for granted a just and effective trial procedure, but does not always specify one. Murray makes suggestions about effective and just trial procedures, suggesting that a defendant's previous convictions for offences similar to those for which he is being tried be admitted as evidence for the prosecution. After all, these previous convictions are relevant to the question of what the defendant is capable of, and, for Murray, trial procedure is either a game or a serious arrangement for finding the truth. I agree that previous convictions are relevant, but they are no substitute for evidence in a case being tried, and there is a substantial danger that juries will allow information about past convictions to fill the gaps in prosecution evidence in the cases they are trying. If that is right, Murray's procedure permits juries to rely on evidence that, while relevant, is not relevant enough. Murray indeed goes further than prior convictions: he wants prior arrests to be brought to the attention of juries (p. 23). Since arrest is much more subject to personal discretion than conviction, it is highly probable that gratuitous or unreasonable arrest would add weight to a prosecution in a case where it should not.

Still, it is a fact, and an important fact, that many crimes are committed by a few criminals, and this needs to be acted upon in the right way in the criminal justice system. Murray thinks the action needs to consist of a reform of rules of evidence at trial; but I wonder why it is not better reflected in powers for the police. People who have committed repeated offences deserve intense surveillance, perhaps by means of electronic tagging, and those who are thinking of embarking on crime should know that they face this surveillance in addition to arrest and prison if they re-offend. This is how repeat offending can be given weight without trials being prejudiced. Those who have most exposure to, and most resources to act on, an offender's past criminal record—the police—are able to do so, with the aim of preventing similar crimes, rather than securing convictions for them. A merit of this suggestion is that surveillance techniques can be justified in cases of Outlawry that consist of repeated taunting and verbal abuse and not just Outlawry in the form of Murray's acts of elemental predation.

If the rules of evidence in criminal trials are not relaxed in the ways that Murray suggests, I have no quarrel, as a nuanced retributivist, with two other provisions of Murray's simple justice: judges should have limited discretion to depart from prescribed penalties, and the punishments should be administered. The justification these tenets of simple justice get from a nuanced retributivism is that the first increases impartiality and that the second is required by any system of penal justice. Murray's approach is selective in its promotion of impartiality, and that is one of its great weaknesses as an approach to justice. But it is right to insist on implementation of the law even when that costs a lot of money.

The Injustice of Simple Justice

Vivien Stern

On 14 December 2004, the Joint Committee on Human Rights of the two Houses of Parliament published a report on deaths in custody. It is a sad catalogue of lost lives. One case, described in the report as 'particularly worrying', is that of Joseph Scholes. According to the report, Joseph, aged 15 at the time, was arrested for peripheral involvement in a series of robberies. At the time of his arrest, he was having suicidal thoughts and had began harming himself. He had a history as a victim of sexual abuse. Two weeks before his court appearance, he slashed his face with a knife over 30 times. He was given a custodial sentence and sent to serve it at Stoke Heath Young Offender Institution. A few days after his sixteenth birthday, and after nine days in the institution, he hanged himself.[1]

I have struggled to find a place for what happened to Joseph Scholes in Charles Murray's ideas about justice. I do not know what he would say in answer to the question, 'Did the retributive justice system do the right thing in relation to Joseph?' The system certainly followed the Murray principles. It put Joseph in the box called 'bad guy' and called down upon him a sentence of punishment recently decreed by the higher judiciary to be appropriate for the act of street-robbery, even though some of those involved must have had misgivings about what they were doing. We know the judge had such severe misgivings that he waited for 19 days after Joseph pleaded guilty before passing sentence. When sentencing him to a two-year detention and training order, the judge stated in open court that he wanted the warnings about Joseph's self-harming and his history of

I am grateful to Helen Fair of the International Centre for Prison Studies for her help with the research for this paper.

being the victim of sexual abuse 'most expressly drawn to the attention of the authorities'.[2] But in spite of such anxieties, in the end the system followed the Murray principles.

I cannot pretend to know what Charles Murray would say about the events that led to the death of Joseph Scholes. His views on other social matters are so controversial that it is hard to see where the fate of a disturbed teenager would fit. Certainly he might well say this should not have happened. He did not intend that his simple justice should be followed that simply.

The case of Joseph Scholes may be a special one. But once we admit one case in which the simple idea is wrong that people can be divided into the wholly good and wholly bad by virtue of whether they have carried out one act for which a fixed or inflexible punishment is due, then we must accept it can be wrong in other cases too. At the very least, the system has to become more questioning in its division of people into good guys and bad guys.

What about Paige Tapp who was sent to prison for threatening violence against the policewoman who prevented her from killing herself? Once in prison, she managed what she had been prevented from doing outside and killed herself there.[3] What about Petra Blanksby? Petra was 18 and had a history of self-harm when she was remanded to prison. During her 130 days in jail she tried to kill herself 92 times, and eventually succeeded. She had no criminal convictions, but did have a proven history of depression and had been harming herself since she was 12 years old. Her actual offence was serious, it was 'arson with intent to endanger life', even though the life was her own. She bought a can of petrol and set herself alight in her council flat. She was found by the emergency services cowering in a doorway, her hair in flames. According to her family, the damage to her flat was so minor that the council did not even want to press charges.[4]

What about what happens 'every afternoon at Wormwood Scrubs' prison according to journalist Nick Davies? At this time, according to him, 'the white prison vans queue up outside the gate, ferrying men back from the courts—the young and surly, the old and confused, the crackhead who was caught shoplifting yet again, the homeless man who set fire to an empty building, the man who thumped a stranger because he looked at him in a funny way, the old Rasta who screams at himself in the park'.[5]

The position is similar in the United States where prisons are increasingly full of the mentally ill. 'About one in six prisoners is mentally ill. A spate of recent studies describe American prisons as mental institutions by default— although they are institutions in which the disturbed prisoners get no treatment to speak of. Once they complete their sentences, they are generally dumped onto the streets without medication or therapy, and rapidly end up back in jail.'[6]

Do not Charles Murray's simple propositions that the world can be divided into good or bad, and that, if bad, punishment must follow, lead to accepting as right the actions of the State of Arkansas in the case of Charles Singleton? Charles Singleton was a diagnosed schizophrenic, 44 years old. Twenty-five years ago he received a death sentence for having murdered a grocery store assistant called Mary Lou York. Since he was mentally ill and the Supreme Court did not permit the execution of mentally ill people, he stayed on death row and his condition worsened. Then, he was forcibly given powerful drugs to alleviate the symptoms. His lawyer appealed against the forcible medication. On 10 February 2003, the Third Circuit Court of Appeals held that the State of Arkansas could continue to medicate Mr Singleton—knowing that the idea was that he should become sane enough to be executed. In January 2004 he was given a lethal injection in the state's death chamber.[7]

So, I am dubious about a conceptual framework where the division into good guys and bad guys leaves so little room for prosecutors and judges to decide what is humane and what is just. I suspect that, if *Sunday Times* readers were asked if they agreed it is a good idea for distressed and mentally ill young people, women or men, to be sent to prison and commit suicide there, few would want to be associated with it.

So, simple justice is too simple for me, when it disregards the circumstances and characteristics of the accused and the circumstances of the act deemed to be criminal. I would prefer Winston Churchill's magnificent formulation. Speaking of penal justice he said that it should be guided by 'an unfaltering faith that there is treasure, if you can only find it, in the heart of every man.'

Charles Murray is also very much in support of the current government policy of making it easier to convict those accused of offences by allowing the jury to hear of previous convictions if they are deemed relevant. When they were first put to the House of Lords in June 2003, plans along the lines advocated by Charles Murray encountered fierce opposition from Conservatives, Liberals, Independents, and some Labour backbenchers. Often the basis of this opposition was a premise with which Charles Murray agrees—*viz*. that this a world where 'states have had an ugly habit of coercing inaccurate confessions' (p. 22). They cannot always be trusted to do the right thing and to follow the rule of law. So, safeguards are needed. The Conservative Front Bench Spokesperson, Baroness Anelay, said that the Government proposals would lead to 'a serious risk of people being convicted on the basis of their past criminal record and not on the basis of the facts of the alleged offence before the court'.[8] The Labour lawyer, Lord Brennan, foresaw that the provisions to allow information about previous convictions to be put before the jury would lead to miscarriages of justice.[9] A former Attorney-General, Lord Mayhew, called the proposals 'too seriously prosecution-minded, at the expense of safeguards for the ordinary person prosecuted by the state...'.[10] Late last year, one of the leading opponents of the Government's policies, Baroness Helena Kennedy QC, observed from its own backbenches in the House of Lords that: 'In a culture where we are all encouraged to think of ourselves as potential victims of criminals or terrorists, we easily forget that the state is capable of victimising us more effectively.'[11]

On this too I find Charles Murray unconvincing. The history of miscarriages of justice in Britain is an inglorious one that has done great damage to the justice system.

James Robinson, Michael Hickey and Vincent Hickey spent 17 years in prison for a crime they did not commit. So did Stefan Kisko. Not only is it a great injustice when an innocent person spends 17 years in prison. It also tarnishes the justice system in the eyes of the public.

Third, I must take issue with Charles Murray's love-affair with imprisonment. The attachment to mass imprisonment as a solution to poverty and economic restructuring is a phenomenon unique to the United States, though other jurisdictions, such as England and Wales, seem not unimpressed with the policy across the Atlantic. However, the United States is still in a class all its own. The average imprisonment rate for the old European Union countries is 108 per 100,000. The countries of the former Soviet Union had very high imprisonment rates, but many of these have reduced significantly. Russia for example has reduced its prison population from 1,060,000 in 2000 to 787,900 in August 2004 and its imprisonment rate is now 548 per 100,000, the third highest in the world. Belarus has a higher rate, 554. No country comes in the 600-700 per 100,000 slot. Only one country in the world has an imprisonment rate above 700 per 100,000 of its general population. That is the United States. This high use of imprisonment is not a North American phenomenon. The imprisonment rate in Canada is 116 per 100,000. The United States has 4.6 per cent of the world's population and 23.1 per cent of the world's prisoners. As a neighbourly comparison, Canada has 0.51 per cent of the world's population and 0.4 per cent of the world's prisoners.

Charles Murray would, it seems, like to advise the United Kingdom to follow the US experiment and put more of its citizens in prison. Although the Government has seen an increase in prison numbers of 25 per cent since it came to power in May 1997, it is unlikely to get the money to bring the prison population up to US levels. Even some US states are beginning to feel the pinch and have started to look for ways to cut their use of prison by introducing alternatives and treatment for many convicted people who would formerly have been locked up.[12] To lock up five times as many people, which would bring us to US levels, would probably cost an additional £10.56 billion. Even if all these new prison places are in privately-built and run prisons, the costs are likely to be almost the same.[13]

Furthermore, even if such a policy appeals to the parts of the Government concerned with the justice system, and it well might, they are unlikely to get the money. This is because those in charge of giving out the money cannot help noticing that prison is very poor value for money. Perhaps it is right to modify that statement a little. Prison is very poor value for money as a device for controlling everyday crime and securing social peace and safe communities where people feel at ease. It is undeniably good value for money when used in the short term instead of a good psychiatric hospital (more expensive at £72,800 per place per year[14]) first-class residential drug treatment (no more expensive at £35,620 per year[15]) or a residential school for a disturbed teenager (much more expensive at around £150,000 a year[16]). But I am assuming that neither Charles Murray nor Civitas are arguing that prison should replace health or social care or educational provision.

In relation to crime control, once prison has fulfilled its purpose as a place of punishment for serious crime and as a place which holds those from whom society needs to be protected, its use above that level is expensive and socially unproductive. The deterrent value of prison sentences and longer rather than shorter sentences cannot be established. The incapacitation effect, that is the crimes not committed by those imprisoned, undoubtedly exists, but is generally reckoned to be small and needs to be set against substitution (e.g. when a drug-dealer is taken off a patch and into prison, the trade is taken over by someone else within a few days) and the additional number of people pushed into crime over time because of being brought up in a family where imprisonment is the norm. So a Chancellor of the Exchequer concerned to use resources well for social betterment and economic growth is unlikely to give money easily for greater use of imprisonment. The results are just not very good when compared with other ways of spending public money. As Mary-Ann Sieghart said in *The Times*: 'We could cut crime dramatically if we were to prescribe heroin to all addicts for free on the NHS and provide substantially more residential places for rehabilitation'.[17]

If *Sunday Times* readers were asked to chose between prison and drug treatment for those whose crime activities stemmed from drug addiction, I suggest a majority would plump for the treatment option. It is not just Chancellors of the Exchequer who see the nonsense of so much negative expenditure. So, too, do local people in the areas from which the bulk of the prison population comes. In December 2003, I went to Brooklyn in New York. A thousand people from Brooklyn came to a conference to talk about solving the problems of crime in their borough. They were not talking about policing and prisons, courts and sentences. They were talking about housing, employment, health, and education; and they were adding up dollars. They had done some geographical plotting. They had analysed where the prisoners lived, where the poor people lived, where the victims lived, where the most social services were needed and were not available in sufficient quantity. They found, not surprisingly, that where the poor people live and where the services are needed is also where the prison population comes from. Some blocks, single streets, consume one million dollars worth of imprisonment in a year. People from those streets are going into prison for short sentences —up to three years (that is a short sentence in the US)— and then coming back.

Now those people in Brooklyn were asking, 'Can we have that money and spend it on the people here, sorting out their problems and getting them to do community service that benefits the neighbourhood instead of sending them to prison?'

Thus there has grown up in the United States a movement called 'Justice Reinvestment', a movement which is working to get much of the money spent on imprisonment away from the prison budget and into the social policy budget, so that there can be drug treatment, work training, business start-up grants and education, in the areas where most of the prisoners come from.

Finally, I am sure some readers will quarrel with my arguments. Such matters as how much crime an undue use of prison prevents and how much crime it creates can be debated endlessly drawing on statistics, as can arguments about which analysis of public opinion to believe. Does the public think prison is a good deal, or not? Some surveys would suggest that they do. Surveys done for the project 'Rethinking Crime and Punishment', carried out by MORI, suggest otherwise. I imagine that in fact the public holds both views simultaneously. Like justice, public opinion also is not as simple as Charles Murray would like it to be. *Sunday Times* readers overwhelmingly agreed with the good guy/bad guy view set out in his questions. Suppose they had been asked my three questions:

1) Should Joseph Scholes have been dealt with in the way he was?
2) Should we have treatment rather than prison for heroin addicts?
3) Is prison a good way of spending money if you want to prevent crime compared with other ways of spending that money?

I suspect I would then have scored quite well too.

Basically, the main differences between Charles Murray's view of justice and that of many of the 'élite people' in the British criminal justice system whom he interviewed are differences of world-view. They differ from him, as do I, on some very basic questions. How much help should the sick, the weak and the abused get compared with how much punishment? How 'good' are those of us who are deemed to be 'good'? How comfortable would it be to live in a society like the United States where more than two million people are imprisoned, where the chance of a black boy going to prison sometime in his life is one in three,[18] and where people are imprisoned for 25 years for shoplifting a baseball glove?[19]

These are deeper ethical and philosophical questions on which Charles Murray is on one side and I am definitely on the other.

Rethinking Crime and Punishment

Rob Allen

Introduction

Charles Murray's latest polemic on the state of criminal justice in the UK seems fuelled by frustration at what he considers the British failure to take on board the lessons from his home country. With two million prisoners, the land of the free leads the world in incarceration, locking up more than one in every 150 of its citizens, at vast economic and social cost. Murray has nothing to say about the disastrous social consequences of American penal policy—the enormous racial disparities involved which give black males born today a one in three chance of going to prison during their lifetime; the impact on the economies of the poorest communities where high numbers of men of working age are locked up at public expense; the collateral damage to families and children of prisoners; or the epidemics of violence, self harm, and mental illness which blight life inside prison. Nor does he say anything about the body of academic work that shows that the recent drop in crime in America is largely the result of social forces other than rising prison numbers and that increasing such numbers is not the most effective means of achieving public safety. Yet mass incarceration is the policy prescription that he urges on the UK.

For Murray, these negative dimensions are seemingly irrelevant to his key message: that we need to wage war on crime in a simple fashion—by 'locking up the bad guys' and protecting the good. Notwithstanding the sharp rise in imprisonment in England and Wales over the last 12 years, our 75,000 prisoners still represents less than a quarter of the American rate of detention. For Murray this is evidence that we are 'reluctant crime fighters', in thrall to a form of progressive justice which sides with the criminal. Combining nostalgia for England in the first half of the twentieth century, a critique of the liberal propensities of the so called 'criminal justice élite' and a forceful exposition of the philosophy of retribution, 'Simple Justice' argues for a quantum change in criminal policy which would see prison numbers tripled or quadrupled, the rights of defendants stripped away and the creation of a new political agenda which gives the public the very much tougher approach which they are supposed to want.

Murray finds it hard to understand why, on this side of the Atlantic, so few of those with responsibilities in criminal justice share his simple philosophy. He cannot find many politicians, lawyers or police officers who espouse the positions he holds—for example, that the prison population should depend on the number of people who commit serious crimes and if that means tripling the prison population so be it; that whether or not prison rehabilitates people is irrelevant in deciding whether an offender should go to prison; or that Tony Martin did nothing wrong.

The reason for what Murray sees as our squeamish approach may be that public leaders have been brought up on Titmuss's nostrum that 'the denial of complexity is the essence of tyranny'. But it may be that, in Britain, there is a well-established view that crime is clearly not just a matter of wickedness or weakness as conservatives claim. And nor is it simply a result of poverty and disadvantage as progressives have sometimes suggested. Individuals' behaviour is the product of a complex mix of personality and situation. We therefore need a system that recognises and responds to that mix, if justice is to be done. At the levels of law, practice, and policy, far from being a simple matter of one size fits all, a fair and effective approach to dealing with crime must take account of the circumstances, needs and differences between individual cases, in a way that 'simple justice' can never do.

The tyranny of simplicity

It is the Tony Martin case that perhaps undermines most clearly the argument for simple justice and illustrates the need for an approach to wrongdoing which takes much fuller account of the range of complex factors at play. In 2000, Mr Martin used an unlicensed gun to take a pot shot at two intruders outside his farmhouse, killing one, a 16-year-old boy, and injuring another. Martin's conviction for murder was overturned on appeal and he received a five-year sentence for manslaughter. Since then there have been calls for a change in the law to give householders immunity from prosecution in such cases. Charles Murray thinks that Martin did nothing wrong and that a change in the law is needed so that people can defend their property in any way they choose without having to worry about the consequences.

There are strong arguments that the current law, which allows *reasonable* force to be used in such circumstances, strikes precisely the right balance between the right to defend property and other socially important values. It is based on a belief which sets the value of life and limb at a higher level than property and a judgement that limiting the availability and use of lethal weapons is a desirable goal in a civilised society. In short, it takes account of the social consequences of the law in a way that Murray would not allow.

In a similar vein, Murray does not appear to think that the impact of imprisonment on an individual offender's likelihood of further offending is relevant when a court decides whether or not an offender should be locked up. According to his logic, if a period in detention demonstrably increases the likelihood of an offender committing a serious violent crime, this would not matter. But surely if people come out of prison worse than they go in, creating a greater risk of re-offending, we should be concerned at the very least to ensure that prison is used only when no other sentence would be adequate. To ensure this is the case would of course require courts to adopt the kind of individualised approach Murray so dislikes.

At a policy level, Murray acknowledges that implementing retributive justice is 'simple but expensive'. It would mean an increase in the prison population 'that dwarfs anything that any politician ... is prepared to countenance'. What he fails to say is *how* much it would cost and how else resources could be deployed in ways that reduce or respond to crime in more socially productive ways. Given the large numbers of mentally ill and drug-addicted people in prison, spending funds on their treatment and rehabilitation is likely to prove a more effective and more humane response than imprisonment. Economic analysis has suggested that intervening early with children at risk can produce better results than prison. The UK Audit Commission reported last year that: 'Many young people who end up in custody have a history of professionals failing to listen, assessments not being followed by action and nobody being in charge. If effective early intervention had been provided for just one in ten of these young offenders, annual savings in excess of £100 million could have been made.' The point that Murray fails to make is that the resources needed to implement his programme would inevitably draw funding away from such early intervention measures.

One of the major problems he has with 'progressive justice'—that it cannot deliver on what it promises—could be resolved if it were funded more realistically.

Specific problems with retributive justice

In addition to the general problem of gross oversimplification, there are three particular problems with Murray's no-nonsense espousal of retributive justice.

Outlaws and Citizens

The first of these particular problems concerns the idea that people should be divided between Citizens and Outlaws—a dichotomous world-view that seems as simplistic as it is disturbing. Murray boldly asserts that the Citizens produce everything good in English life and that priority must be given to their protection. Those who commit serious crimes—murder, rape, robbery and burglary, 'the elemental predatory acts'—should be treated as Outlaws, forfeiting many of the rights enjoyed by the law abiding.

The language of the Wild West and Old Testament may appeal to American sensibilities, but, ironically, it is in this country, where the Christian church is established and we are all subjects rather than citizens, that the values of mercy, forgiveness, and tolerance seem to play a greater role. Research on the kinds of people who become serious and persistent offenders has been remarkably consistent in many countries of the world. They are drawn from the poor, the ill-educated, the drug-addicted, the abused and neglected, people who have little stake in conformity. Many have serious mental health problems. This does not always excuse their crimes. But it is a context, which cannot be wished away by those who make a socially responsible criminal justice policy. It points to precisely the kinds of measure which are needed if crime is to be reduced. Of course, those who commit crimes need to be held to account for what they have done, and, it is argued below, need to be given every opportunity and encouragement to put things right by their victim and the wider community. Organising a response to their offending on the basis that, as people, they are outside the law is both morally questionable and practically unhelpful. The moral problem arises from defining human beings solely in terms of their behaviour. Are people who do bad things automatically bad people who need to be defined and labelled as such? Police officers, whose no nonsense approach is much approved of by Murray, often talk about villains and bad guys as if people cannot change and cannot redeem themselves. What would Murray make of Jimmy Boyle, once Scotland's most notorious criminal, now a successful artist? Or the long-term prisoners who work in a Citizens Advice Bureau in Oxford; or the man who heroically saved dozens in the Far East Tsunami before being arrested for burglary on his return to Australia?

The practical problem arises from the fact that treating people as Outlaws makes it more difficult for them to change their ways. Work undertaken for Rethinking Crime and Punishment (RCP) on the economic costs of crime has highlighted the heavy reputational costs of a criminal record. Discharged prisoners find it difficult to rent a house, get a job or a credit card—the kind of market-exclusion effects that may be more debilitating than a term of imprisonment itself.

Sentenced prisoners cannot vote in elections. And those with a criminal record are unable to claim from the Criminal Injuries Compensation board. A sensible crime policy would aim to reduce the disparities between Citizens and Outlaws, not enshrine them.

Progressive justice

The second particular issue relates to the dimensions of justice. For Murray, the primal function of a system of justice is to depersonalise revenge by making society responsible for the punishment of culpable offenders. Murray's Hobbesian view may be of historical interest, but how relevant is it to modern societies? While, for Murray, punishment is the be-all and end-all, progressive justice aims to achieve other objectives. The punishment of offenders is only one of the five purposes of sentencing to which the courts in England and Wales must have regard. Murray would presumably approve of two of the other purposes—the reduction of crime (including its reduction by deterrence) and the protection of the public. But it is the other two—the reform and rehabilitation of offenders, and the making of reparation by offenders to persons affected by their offences—that distinguish justice from revenge. Restorative Justice (RJ) in particular provides a much more comprehensive and constructive approach to crime than that propounded by Murray. Borrowing heavily from mediation routinely used in civil disputes, RJ provides an opportunity for offenders to take responsibility for the loss, damage or harm they have caused and do something to make amends. RJ allows victims to let the offender know how the crime affected them and put a bad experience behind them. Pilot schemes are showing that victims who participate in RJ are much more satisfied than they are with conventional criminal justice.

Murray is right that, in these forms of more progressive justice, deciding on a just sentence for a convicted offender is a far from simple matter. It requires careful and intelligent assessment of the factors relating to the offence and the offender and a balanced judgement about the best measures to impose. For Murray, these may be noble aspirations but are impossible to achieve in practice, because we lack effective mechanisms for diagnosing and treating underlying problems. It is true that the 1,700 residential drug rehabilitation places in England represent a major shortfall. The answer is surely to expand these and other services using the considerable resources Murray would have us tie up in prisons.

Murray asks us to consider that it is difficult enough for parents to decide how best to deal with a misbehaving child whom they know well, let alone for a judge to assess and treat an offender about whom they have virtually no information. The analogy is instructive. Good parents know that bringing up children is as much about praise as punishment. When their children steal something or harm someone, the priority is to get them to apologise and put the harm right. When choosing between the options for correction, parents would not consider doing anything which would inflict damage or harm on their child. Murray does not explain what he means by 'a lesson that won't soon be forgotten', but it is sobering that, in the country which invented the juvenile court to act as 'a kind and just parent', 2,000 juveniles are today detained for life without the possibility of parole.

Public attitudes

The third issue relates to public attitudes. Lord Bingham recently summed up the position when he said, 'Everybody thinks our system is becoming soft and wimpish. In point of fact it's one of the most punitive systems in the world.' For Murray, the criminal justice élites are out of touch with public opinion, which favours the simple justice approach; they live in different worlds. But work carried out for the RCP has found that, although public attitudes are complex, sometimes contradictory, and often highly dependent on the wording of poll questions, in general they are much less punitive than is often thought to be the case.

First, it is clear that there is a good deal of support for prevention. Asked to choose from a list of options two or three measures which would do most to reduce crime in Britain, 60 per cent of people say better parenting, 55 per cent more police, 45 per cent better school discipline, and 41 per cent more constructive activities for young people. When we asked in 2001 how the public would spend a notional £10 million on dealing with crime, the most popular option was to set up teams in 30 cities to work with children at risk. Nearly three-quarters of people think schools and colleges have an important role in preventing young people from offending and re-offending, with teachers seen as more important in this regard than police, courts or custody. This confirms the findings of an EU-wide survey in 2002, which found more support for targeted prevention programmes than for tougher sentencing.

Second, there is a great deal of scepticism about prison. About half of the members of the public surveyed think that offenders come out of prison worse than they go in and a third don't know. Only two per cent chose to spend the notional £10 million on prison places. When asked how to deal with prison overcrowding, building more prisons is the least popular option, with the support of only a quarter of people. This reflects the finding that only one in ten people think putting more offenders in prison would do most to reduce crime in Britain.

Third, there is a desire for better alternatives. To deal with prison overcrowding, more than half of the public would prefer tougher community punishments to be developed. Nine out of ten of those surveyed agree that there should be more use of intensive community punishments to keep track of young offenders. Focus group research by Strathclyde University found that people want non-custodial sentences that make offenders pay back and learn their lesson. Research on the reputation of alternatives to prison found a need to benefit victims, communities and offenders.

Fourth, there is support for treating rather than punishing underlying problems. More than half of the public think that the best way of dealing with prison overcrowding is to build more residential centres so that drug-addicted offenders can receive treatment. In focus group research, 'almost all respondents, including tabloid readers, adopted liberal positions on the issue of drug crime and felt strongly that drug users should be treated rather than punished'. For young offenders, education is seen as playing an important role. Two-thirds of people agree (a third strongly) that under-18s who have offended and cannot read and write should receive compulsory education rather than custody.

These four findings might seem to be somewhat at odds with the prevailing wisdom, including Murray's, about public attitudes. Evidence from some opinion polls suggests that people in Britain have harsher attitudes towards offenders than RCP's work suggests. It is true that, when asked if they want stiffer sentences, seven out of ten people will say 'yes', and that between a quarter and a third will 'strongly agree' that the courts are 'too lenient'. Moreover, three-quarters of people think that the police and the courts are 'too lenient' when dealing with young offenders. However, it is well established that people simply do not know how severe the system actually is in terms of the use and the length of custodial sentences. For example, the Home Office has found that over half of people make large underestimates of the proportion of adults convicted of rape, burglary and mugging who go to prison, and recent research conducted for the Sentencing Advisory Panel confirmed this picture. Nearly three-quarters of people believed that sentences for domestic burglary were 'too lenient', and nearly half that they were 'much too lenient'. However, people consistently underestimated the degree to which courts actually imposed prison sentences. Close analysis would suggest that there is something of a 'comedy of errors' in which policy and practice are not based on a proper understanding of public opinion, and public opinion is not based on a proper understanding of policy and practice. As the Home Office put it, 'tough talk does not necessarily mean a more punitive attitude to sentencing'.

Implications for policy

The Blair Government's proposals to mark the end of the 'liberal consensus' on law and order and further move justice away from defendants and in favour of 'victims' would seem to go nowhere near far enough for Murray. He would doubtless approve of the crackdown on anti-social behaviour, which is propelling more and more social misfits into prison, and of the promise to give householders greater rights to defend their property by force. But how liberal is our system and how far does it need rebalancing?

There is no doubt that sentencing of offenders has become very much tougher in recent years. There are 30,000 more people in prison than when Tony Blair became Labour leader ten years ago, costing the Treasury an extra billion pounds each year. Research carried out for RCP found that this does not reflect an increase in crime—recorded crime is at its lowest level since 1984—nor a rise in the numbers sentenced. Nor, as far as we can tell, are offences more serious. It is simply that judges and magistrates are imposing longer prison sentences for serious crimes and are more likely to imprison offenders who ten years ago would have received a community penalty or even a fine. Their collective decisions reflect an increasingly punitive climate of political and media debate about crime.

Charles Murray thinks that the difference between élite and public opinion on crime is a chasm, with open-ended implications for political realignment. The work of RCP suggests the need for such realignment but along a very different trajectory from Murray's. An alternative approach, which would cut the number of victims, would be to give much greater priority to preventing youngsters offending in the first place and treating the hard drug addicts who make up more than half of those arrested.

Alongside this, the Government should invest in restorative justice and other kinds of problem-solving approaches. Research for RCP has found substantial public support for an approach based on getting offenders to pay back rather than punish them. Shifting the balance of the system in this

direction is the way forward, together with serious investment in the education, health and social programmes which
can reduce the numbers of both victims and offenders.

Conclusion

Nietzsche's warning to 'Distrust all in whom the urge to
punish is strong' applies with particular force to Charles
Murray. His pessimistic view of human nature and extremely conservative attitude to the role of government
combine to produce a bleak and repressive vision which is
as unsuited to this country as it is undesirable. Despite a
sharp movement to the right in recent years, there remains
in Britain some sense of social solidarity and a commitment
to combating social exclusion, even where offenders are
concerned. But there are dangers that some at least of the
thinking underpinning 'Simple Justice' is making headway
with both Labour and Conservative politicians. The chal-
lenge for progressives is not only to highlight the negative
consequences of the kind of penal maximalism outlined by
Charles Murray, but to articulate a politically viable vision
for criminal justice based on hope as much as it is on fear.

A Plague on Both Your Statist Houses:
Why Libertarian Restitution Beats State-Retribution and State-Leniency

J.C. Lester

Charles Murray describes himself as a libertarian, most notably in his short book *What it Means to be a Libertarian*.[1] He might more accurately have described himself as having libertarian tendencies. My reading of 'Simple Justice' is that the views it espouses are far more traditionalist than libertarian. Neither traditionalist state-retribution nor modernist state-leniency is libertarian. Nor does either provide as just or efficient a response to crime as does libertarian restitution, including restitutive retribution. Here, I shall respond directly only to Murray's views, rather than also deal with state-leniency. This is because I accept Murray's thesis, without endorsing his specific arguments for it, that state-leniency is disastrous as a response to crimes against persons and their justly acquired property.

It is shocking and disgusting to see states today give violators of persons and property the upper hand, while they commit their crimes, throughout the judicial procedure after apprehension and during their trials, and in their final sentencing upon being convicted. The offensiveness of this country's criminal justice system is compounded by the gross inefficiency of state policing here. However, to agree with Murray about the injustice and inefficiency of the current way of dealing with crime is about as far as a libertarian can really go. In commenting on Murray's paper,

This essay is far clearer than it otherwise would have been thanks to critical responses from Mark Brady, David Conway, David Goldstone and David McDonagh.

I shall outline a radical and genuinely progressive libertarian option. In so doing, I recognise, and make no apology for the fact, that I stand at the extreme end of the libertarian spectrum.

Who needs the state?

According to those who occupy my preferred end of the libertarian spectrum, states serve no useful purposes, including the maintenance of law and order, that could not be achieved more effectively and justly by private and purely voluntary agencies and associations, created and maintained out of the uncoerced actions of ordinary private individuals acting only from self-interest and the dictates of their consciences.[2] Throughout, I use 'libertarian' in this extreme sense, although there are also minimal-state libertarians. I shall begin by briefly outlining my own libertarian conception of crime and of the way in which it should be treated, with which even most radical libertarians may disagree, and without offering very much by way of clarification or criticism of it.[3]

The origins of law may be traced to anarchically evolved, and ever-evolving, enforceable rules of conduct specifying how people must behave to avoid aggressing against the persons or justly acquired property of others.[4] Acts that intentionally or recklessly aggress against the persons or property of others—and which tend thereby to add indignity and fear—constitute the only 'crimes' there are in the libertarian sense of that word. That there are no real 'victimless' crimes—for instance, producing and selling state-banned medications or recreational drugs—is a key libertarian tenet Murray fails even to mention.

In the libertarian view, there is no necessary connection between law and crime, on the one hand, and what a state decides to command or forbid by way of conduct, on the other. A state may forbid conduct not at all criminal in the libertarian sense, and it may permit conduct that is criminal. Indeed, from the libertarian perspective, states themselves notoriously authorise and engage in forms of criminal conduct, most notably taxation (systematic extortion) and aggressive war (mass murder). Note that this evolved-law thesis asserts not merely that such state 'law' and activity is immoral, but that it is not really law or legal at all. A type of conduct no more becomes legal or illegal simply because the state says so, than it becomes moral or immoral because it does. Nor does anyone's command become law simply because he has the power to enforce it.

Whenever there has taken place a genuine crime in the libertarian sense of the term, then there is some victim of it whose person or justly acquired property has been proactively imposed on in some way by another person and who, in consequence, enjoys against that perpetrator of the crime a just claim to full restitution for the disvalue sustained as a result of its perpetration—in principle, at least, for it might not always be practical or possible to extract it. Thus, libertarian criminal law and civil law overlap. All crimes require restitution, but not all legal restitution is owed because of a crime. Perpetrators of crime owe their victims as restitution more than whatever would fully compensate for whatever proximate damage or loss their victims suffer to their person or property, including any feelings of shock or fear they suffer as a result of these crimes. In addition, perpetrators of crime owe their victims restitution for the additional risk to which they put them that they might not be able to recover any restitution because their assailant manages to escape conviction. I call this latter variable the 'risk-multiplier'.

The risk-multiplier

For example, if there is only a one-in-ten chance perpetrators of a given kind of crime are apprehended and convicted, then full restitution to victims of it involves their perpetrators having to cede to their victims something of equal value to the value of the proximate loss each suffers to person or property, multiplied by ten. This is precisely what victims require to receive from their assailants to take account of the risk that was imposed on them.[5] Only to require criminals to make restitution for whatever proximate damage they cause their victims would mean they are allowed to impose on their victims, without having to make any restitution for it, the often far greater disvalue they cause their victims by the risk that they might escape.[6]

Consider a different kind of case from the risk-multiplier, but one that clarifies the disvalue of imposed risks as such. Suppose someone imposes on your head a game of Russian roulette in which the gun does not fire, although there was a one-in-six chance it might have done. Surely you are owed not just for any fear, etc. to which you were subjected, which, in this instance, forms the proximate damage you were made to suffer, and which might have been relatively small had the episode occurred very suddenly or even without your knowing at the time. You are surely also owed an additional amount, probably much higher and possibly infinite, that it would be reasonable of you to demand from anyone who sought to impose that risk on you. Similarly, someone caught and convicted of a crime should not be let off having to provide his victim with restitution for the risk he had imposed on him that he might, *ex ante*, have got away with his crime.[7]

Insuring against crime

However, the full debts perpetrators of crime owe their victims in restitution for their crimes are debts the victims might have chosen, in anticipation they might become victims, to 'sell' on to insurance companies through taking out policies against any losses sustained by becoming a victim of such (or any) crimes. Victims might also be able literally to sell the restitution owed them after they have fallen victim to a crime. In either case, victims of crime would acquire against their insurers a claim for a sum that would fully compensate them for any proximate disvalue suffered, but which takes no, or only partial, account of the risk-multiplier. Whether or by how much it did would depend on the precise terms of their contract.

Those who take out such policies might be able to guarantee they receive compensation should they ever fall a victim of crime, even if its perpetrators are never detected. Meanwhile, their insurance companies will have acquired from their clients a claim, should they become victims of crime, against their assailants for recovery of the full debt they owe their clients. This full debt they owe includes what is generated by the risk-multiplier. The difference between what companies pay out to their clients in compensation for becoming victims of crime and what the companies thereby become owed by its perpetrators provides them with the inducement to take over these debts that criminals, in the first instance, owe their victims.

If mere financial compensation were the only form in which restitution could be demanded by victims, people who wished to commit crime would effectively be able to purchase a licence to do so. Should victims prefer, they should be able to obtain 'restitutive retribution'.[8] This is exacted by criminals being made to suffer as much personal injury or pain as they caused their victims magnified by any risk-multiplier. If you twist my arm, as though it were your property to use as you wish and in doing so break it, you thereby cede me a reciprocal right to break yours, or else for me to have it broken by an agent acting for me. This might look like retribution pure and simple. Where is the literal restitution, or restoration, in my breaking your arm? However, suppose the restitution owing to me in monetary terms is £100,000. Should I prefer to take some fraction of that sum in the form of some reciprocal treatment of you, then that is simply how I choose to spend that much of the restitution I am owed. Alternatively, I might prefer to take all my compensation in money and buy a car instead, but that would not 'restore' my arm to not being broken either. You cannot complain that I am proactively imposing on you or imposing to a greater degree than you had imposed on me. Proactive impositions and reactions in excess of the risk-multiplier are all that this libertarian theory disallows.

Competing private agencies are far more likely to be able to catch and prosecute genuine criminals without becoming corrupted in the process than are state institutions, which maintain monopolies in this domain by aggressive violence. Moreover, competing private insurance companies are more likely than states to ensure that victims of crime receive quick and adequate compensation. The large amounts owing as a result of the risk-multiplier might be thought to create the moral hazard of inviting fabrication of evidence, whether by individuals or institutions. However, it must be remembered the risk-multiplier also applies in cases of any large sums fraudulently claimed. In addition, most claims will be sold on to insurance companies which stand to lose all custom if found fraudulent in this way, if not simply wiped out immediately by having to pay any risk-multiplier debt.

From a libertarian perspective, therefore, the key deficiency in Murray's account is the false dichotomy it poses between, on the one hand, retribution in the sense of punishment and, on the other, leniency. The libertarian position, by contrast, is one that embodies restitution for crime, where this is understood as criminals having to repay their victims amounts equal in value to whatever overall losses they have caused—although, as we have seen, victims may choose to obtain restitution in a retributive way. I should add that Murray also fails to distinguish, and then reconcile, deontological and consequentialist arguments for retribution.

In none of the seven hypothetical scenarios that Murray offers to test the moral proclivities of his readers (pp. 7-8) does he include among the possible options an explicitly libertarian response. If, in all the relevant hypothetical scenarios save the last, restitution is put in place of punishment, a libertarian can happily answer '3' to all the questions that Murray asks about them. The final hypothetical scenario concerns the legitimacy of forcibly injecting a criminal-suspect with a truth drug. In this case, to force a suspect not yet found guilty to take such a drug, without at least his having previously entered into some contractual obligation to submit to one upon suspicion, is itself a case of proactively imposing upon someone, and thus a crime in the libertarian sense. Moreover, when libertarian restitution is substituted for punishment, it becomes difficult to see why opting for '3' in any of the other cases qualifies as being 'tough', the adjective Murray uses to describe the attitudes of those likely to choose that option. What is so tough about thinking victims of crime qualify for receiving from their assailants full restitution and ought to receive it, if often only indirectly via insurance companies?

Is the state a community?

Murray claims '[t]he primal function of a system of justice is to depersonalise revenge ... [T]he individual will take his complaint to the community. In return, the community will exact the appropriate retribution—partly on behalf of the wronged individual, but also to express the community's moral values (pp. 18-19). What is said here seems wrong on many levels. Justice does not have an 'essence' or 'primary function' that simply needs to be cited to succeed thereby in refuting all competing conceptions of justice. If retribution is superior to restitution, Murray needs to argue for that thesis. Individual victims of crime may need the support of others, but why should they be entitled to receive it from 'the community'? Murray appears to use this term as a euphemism for the state. However, whereas the state is an organisation (and, in the eyes of libertarians, a criminal one), a community is not. Nor is a community a moral agent, so it has no 'moral values'. Only individuals have these. Why cannot private agencies be able to assist wronged persons better than states, as has been argued by many libertarian theorists, not least by Bruce Benson?[9]

On behalf of his position, Murray cites the Kantian thought-experiment that asks whether a murderer should be executed if his execution served no purpose other than 'pure justice' (p. 19). Kant and Murray say he should be. Libertarians say the correct answer is to be found in the victim's legal defence contract or in his will, or in his known or likely opinion or in the decision of his heirs or other relevantly assigned persons, although it is doubtful many would want to let the murderer off. It is not up to 'the community'—that is, the state—to decide.

Murray is similarly wrong when later on he explicitly states that victims 'do not have the moral right to abrogate the community's obligation to punish wrong behaviour' (p. 20). In the event a victim of some crime genuinely wishes to receive no restitution from his assailant, then, assuming there has been no intimidation of the victim by the criminal etc., that should be his or her choice, however foolish most other people might find it. In a sense, the victim retroactively consents to undergoing whatever the criminal has inflicted on him. In these circumstances, whoever exacts 'retribution' on behalf of that victim or 'the community' initiates a crime against the aggressor who has been forgiven by his victim. Such injustices are the sorts of thing that typically occur when statists attempt to take the law into their own hands in the name of 'the community' or society. From a libertarian point of view, however, there is nothing unjust in people choosing to ban, boycott or berate anyone for any reason at all, provided in so acting they proceed in accordance with private property rules. Hence, provided they conform with these rules, people may take such action against anyone whose behaviour they regard as despicable, although whoever it is might have escaped and be able to escape successful prosecution for acting as he has done. For instance, many might for such a reason choose to ban someone from their private property and policing companies might even refuse to protect such a person.

Murray explains the 'core tenets' of retributive justice as follows:

> The necessary and sufficient justification for punishing criminals is that they did something for which they deserve punishment. 'Something' refers to the behaviours that society has defined as offences. 'Deserve' means that the offenders are culpable—morally responsible. Society not only has the right but the duty to punish culpable offenders. (p. 20)

Again, from a libertarian perspective, what Murray claims here is open to all sorts of question. What right has 'society' to define what does and does not count as an offence, when all that is here meant by 'society' is some state run according to the rules of elected oligarchs? It is, objectively, an offence, as the opposite of a defence, for anyone knowingly to impose proactively on the person or justly acquired property of someone else. If people merely defend them-

selves or their property against such impositions, they are
not guilty of any offences against anyone. The state itself
commits crimes when it attempts to impose on people
things that conflict with protecting persons and their
property. How and why should anyone be 'culpable' if they
seek to evade such arbitrary impositions? The state is not
'society', a term which denotes the free and spontaneous
association of people. Nor has a state the right to punish
anyone, even if a victim wants it to do so. For the
opportunity-cost of its so doing is to exclude the possibility
of the superior market system that would operate without
the state's extortion of resources through taxation and
inflation of the money supply, the two principal sources of
the state's revenue.

Who needs judges?

Why should it be supposed, as Murray appears to, that, in
all criminal cases, there is need of 'jurors' or 'judges'?
Murray only supposes this because he is thinking entirely
within the traditionalist statist framework of law and order.
It is hard in advance to know what different methods of
securing and administering criminal justice would evolve
were the market allowed to operate here. On-the-spot
payments for relatively minor crimes, as even the present
British government has recently suggested for shoplifting
although not as restitution, need not be either inefficient or
an easy option, especially given the risk-multiplier element.

In defending the admissibility in court of the past
criminal record of an accused on trial, something with
which I cannot disagree, Murray interestingly suggests that
'[d]ivinely accurate retributive justice would not punish for
the one burglary out of dozens when the burglar got caught,
but for the aggregate harm that the burglar has done' (p.
25). This is effectively what criminals are being asked to
provide as restitution when what they are computed as
owing takes into account the risk-multiplier. Its extraction
would feel to the criminal like he was being punished for all
the times he was not caught as well. Moreover, what the

criminal will be deemed to owe for his crime will, through using the risk-multiplier, often be a lot more severe than state punishment currently is. Only the exaction of this form of restitution maximises the chances that 'crime does not pay' which is Murray's expressed desire in his final endnote. In principle, it will, typically, not be worth committing any crime because its potential benefits will be at least negated by its potential losses, and any other efforts and expenses will make it even less attractive. We should certainly see the crime level drop back again, and to far lower levels than obtained even in the 1950s to which Murray likes to hark back. We would only see the risk-multiplier fall if proportionally more criminals were brought to book.

Like many traditionalists, Murray is keen on prison. He writes, '[i]n modern England, the only authentic punishment for modern felonies is imprisonment' (p. 25). Prison is indeed a serious punishment. But it is both Draconian and unnecessarily expensive for the most part, while being too lenient in extreme cases. Unless someone poses so great a risk to others that he is likely to do more damage than he could ever pay in restitution, or else he refuses to pay restitution (non-contractual bankruptcy cannot be an option), there is no need for his incarceration. Such extreme cases are relatively few and far between and will be all the more so once criminals see that full risk-multiplier restitution will be enforced. In any case, since, in a libertarian world, prisoners will be obliged to pay their way in prison, being obliged to work there if they want to be fed, there is no need to worry about the expense of maintaining them whilst incarcerated in private prisons. However, for many lesser criminals, mere electronic tagging would at most be necessary or else some other, more inventive, option that only competition is likely to evolve efficiently. And these would provide more cost-effective and more humane alternatives to prison.

In the small minority of cases in which huge debts are owing that are unlikely to be paid by ordinary work, then extreme measures must be taken to recover them. These would still not be punishment but remain the enforcement of restitution. What I am proposing might sound harsh. But the only alternative is to allow the guilty to get away with their crimes against the innocent, which is surely harsher and completely unjust. Sometimes, a crime will be too great for full restitution to be possible, either in terms of property damage (malicious computer viruses often cause this) or personal damage, even a single murder, let alone bombing innocent civilians for political reasons. In these cases, we shall at least have done the best we can.

Overall, Murray's traditionalist-retribution might be less bad than is the existing modernist-leniency that offers even less by way of just and efficient deterrence. However, in arguing for it, Murray entirely overlooks a third option more just, progressive and efficient than either. This is the way of dealing with crime through enforcing libertarian-restitution as the appropriate response to it. Murray must have read enough libertarian literature to be aware of this third option. It is a pity he chose not to consider it in his essay.

Notes

Charles Murray
1: England's Reluctant Crime Fighters

1   Valerie Ruppel posted her story on an internet discussion
    group affiliated with America's *National Review* magazine.

2   Murray, C., *Charles Murray and the Underclass: The
    Developing Debate*, London: IEA Health and Welfare Unit in
    association with the *Sunday Times*, Choice in Welfare No. 33,
    1996.

2: The Case for Simple Justice

1   Kant, I., *The Metaphysical Elements of Justice*, (1780)
    translated by Ladd, J., Indianapolis: Bobbs-Merrill, reprint,
    1965, p. 102.

2   Moore, M.S., *Placing Blame: A Theory of Criminal Law*,
    Oxford: Oxford University Press, 1997.

3   I use the qualifier 'collateral view' because retributive justice
    in its technical philosophical sense does not get into the nuts
    and bolts of policy. As far as I can determine, the 'Citizens
    versus Outlaws' mindset that I describe is essential to
    making retributive justice work, but I welcome contrary
    arguments that the 'We are all sinners on a continuum'
    mindset is also co-ordinate with the implementation of
    retributive justice.

4   For an analysis of where the system breaks down, see
    Murray, C., *Does Prison Work?*, London: IEA Health and
    Welfare Unit, 1997, pp. 6–12.

5   This estimate is reached by first determining the 1954 ratio
    of prisoners to serious crimes. The numerator is the prison
    population for 1954, as reported in the Home Office's annual
    publication, *Prison Statistics England and Wales*. The
    denominator is the sum of 1954 notifiable offences for
    murder, attempt to murder, manslaughter, infanticide,
    wounding or other acts of endangering life, rape of females,
    robbery, and total burglary, as reported in the Home Office's
    annual publication *Crime in England and Wales* (formerly
    entitled *Criminal Statistics England and Wales*). The 1954
    ratio was .2858. The same categories of notifiable offences
    were summed for 2001/2002 (the Home Office stopped using
    the calendar year as the basis for aggregating statistics in
    1997). Note that none of the categories of crime used for this

calculation have been affected by recent changes in police recording of crimes, nor by changes in the definition of a crime. This sum (1,027,199 offences) was multiplied by the 1954 ratio, producing an estimated prison population of 293,573. This number should be treated as an illustration of the order of magnitude of the prison population that would be produced by mimicking practice in 1954. It could be affected by a variety of factors.

Some of those factors could mean that 293,529 is an overestimate. In any given year the number of notifiable offences is accounted for by a certain number of offenders. The ratio of offences to offenders can be interpreted as a 'crimes per criminal' figure. If that ratio rose between 1954 and 2002, then the system would not need to maintain the same ratio of incarcerations to crimes to put the same proportion of criminals behind bars. We have no direct way of knowing what those numbers are. As a way of inferring the direction the ratio has been moving, a study of court appearances for England and Wales is useful Prime, J., White, S., Liriano, S. and Patel, K., 'Criminal Careers of Those Born between 1953 and 1978, England and Wales' (London: Home Office Statistical Bulletin, 12 March 2001). It permits the calculation of the percentage of court appearances that any given percentage of the population accounts for. I have used six per cent of the male population as my benchmark, following the classic study of Philadelphia males born in 1945, which found that six per cent accounted for more than half of all male delinquencies and two-thirds of all violent offences. (Wolfgang, M.E., Figlio, R.M. and Sellin, T. *Delinquency in a Birth Cohort*, Chicago: University of Chicago Press, 1972.) The birth years reported in Prime *et al.* (2001) are 1953, 1958, 1963, 1968, 1973, and 1978. I used court appearances occurring before the age of 21 (Table 5a), and estimated that six per cent of the male population accounted for approximately the following percentages of court appearances for those birth cohorts: 63 per cent, 61 per cent, 65 per cent, 66 per cent, 74 per cent, and 75 per cent respectively. Interpreting these numbers is difficult because of differences in court practice over the decades covered and also because we are extrapolating from court appearances to total offending, but the results are at least consistent with the hypothesis that the ratio representing offences per offender has been rising.

On the other side of the ledger, it is plausible that even going to 293,000 prisoners will not produce the same effects on crime that the imprisonment ratio of 1954 produced. I have not discussed the practical effects of retributive justice in this paper—the topic is justice, not expediency—but obviously a low crime rate is one of the benefits one would hope to produce through a vast increase in imprisonment. But while is easy to maintain a low crime rate with a high rate of imprisonment, as prevailed in both Britain and the United States through the 1950s, cutting crime by increasing imprisonment rates after they have been permitted to fall for an extended period of time is difficult. Readers of a certain age will remember the saying 'Crime doesn't pay' as something that was said seriously. Now imagine trying to get back to a situation in which the people of Britain don't break into laughter when someone says 'Crime doesn't pay.' Maintaining norms is easier than reestablishing norms. Thus the United States has increased the likelihood of imprisonment to nearly the same rates that prevailed in the 1950s. Crime has fallen substantially, but not nearly to 1950s levels. In this sense, the 293,000 figure is probably an underestimate.

Commentaries

Christie Davies

1   Hood, R. and Roddam, A., 'Crime, Sentencing and Punishment', in Halsey, A.H. and Webb, J., *Twentieth Century Social Trends*, Basingstoke: Macmillan, 2000, pp. 675-709.

2   Stephen, J.F., 'Variations in the Punishment of Crime', *The Nineteenth Century*, XVII, 1885, pp. 755-76.

3   Davies, C. and Trivizas, E., 'A neo-Paretian model of discourse about penal policy: basic sentiments and public argument, in *Revue Européenne des Sciences Sociales*, Tome 32, No. 99, 1994 pp. 147-67.

4   Brandon, R. and Davies, C., *Wrongful Imprisonment*, London: Allen and Unwin, 1973.

5   Paley, Archdeacon William, (1785) *Principles of Moral and Political Philosophy*, Indianapolis: Liberty Fund, 2002.

6   Brandon and Davies, *Wrongful Imprisonment*, 1973, pp. 24-46; Frank, Jerome and Barbara, *Not Guilty*, London: Gollancz, 1957, p. 61; Koosed, M.M., 'The Proposed Innocence Protection Act Won't – Unless it also Curbs Mistaken Eye

Witness Identifications', Ohio: *State Law Journal*, Vol. 63, No. 1, 2002, pp. 263-314.

7   Brandon and Davies, *Wrongful Imprisonment*, 1973 pp. 132-40; Kalven, H. and Zeisel, H., *The American Jury*, Boston: Little Brown, 1966, Appendix C, pp. 514-16.

8   Huff, C.R., Rattner, A. and Sagarin, E., *Convicted but Innocent: Wrongful Conviction and Public Policy*, Newbury Park, CA: Sage Publications, 1996, p. 75.

9   Koosed, 'The Proposed Innocence Protection Act Won't – Unless it also Curbs Mistaken Eye Witness Identifications', 2002.

10 Davies, C., *The Strange Death of Moral Britain*, New Brunswick, NJ: Transaction, 2004, pp. 3-27.

11 Davies, *The Strange Death of Moral Britain*, 2004, pp. 29 & 61.

12 Davies, C., 'Can high taxation be enforced?', in Seldon, A. (ed.), *Tax Avoision*, London: Institute of Economic Affairs, 1979, pp. 60-73.

13 Neal, M. and Davies, C., *The Corporation under Siege*, London: Social Affairs Unit, 1998, p. 38.

14 Hough, M. and Mayhew, P., *The British Crime Survey*, First Report, London: HMSO, 1983, pp. 9-14.

15 Davies, C., 'The Criminals' Charter', *The Lawyer*, Vol. 7, Issue 4, 6 April1993.

16 Anderson, D., *The Dictionary of Dangerous Words*, London: Social Affairs Unit, 2000.

John Cottingham

1   *Metaphysics of Morals* [1797], *Tugendlehre*, §36.

2   *Metaphysics of Morals: Rechtslehre*, Part II, §49E.

3   *Philosophie des Rechts*, 1833.

Tom Sorell

1   See my *Moral Theory and Capital Punishment*, Oxford: Blackwell, 1987; 'Aggravated Murder and Capital Punishment', *Journal of Applied Philosophy*, 10, 1993, pp. 73-85. 'Punishment in a Kantian Framework' in Matravers, M. (ed.), *Punishment and Political Theory*, Oxford: Hart

Publishing, 1999, pp. 10-27. 'Two Ideals and the Death Penalty', *Criminal Justice Ethics*, 21, 2002, pp. 27-34.

Vivien Stern

1   House of Lords House of Commons Joint Committee on Human Rights, *Deaths in Custody: Third Report of Session 2004-5*, Vol. 1.

2   *Deaths in Custody: Third Report of Session 2004-5*, Vol. 1.

3   Frith, Maxine, 'I promised her a visit... The next time I saw her was in the morgue', *Independent*, 26 April 2004.

4   Midgley, Carol, 'Why was my self-destructive daughter sent to prison?', *The Times*, 26 November 2004.

5   Davies, Nick, 'Scandal of society's misfits dumped in jail', *Guardian*, 6 December 2004.

6   'The Price of Prisons', *New York Times*, 26 June 2004.

7   'Mentally ill man executed in US', BBC News, 7 January 2004.

8   House of Lords, *Hansard*, 16 June 2003, col. 567.

9   House of Lords, *Hansard*, 16 June 2003, col. 592.

10 House of Lords, *Hansard*, 16 June 2003, col. 612.

11 Kennedy, Helena, 'For Blair there is no such thing as legal principle', *Guardian*, 27 November 27 2004.

12 Schiraldi, Vincent and Greene, Judith, 'Cutting prison costs is tempting in times of fiscal crisis', *San Diego Union-Tribune*, 27 February 2002.

13 *The Operational Performance of PFI prisons: Report by the Comptroller and Auditor General*, National Audit Office, 18 June 2003.

14 From Department of Health figures.

15 From National Treatment Agency figures.

16 Benjamin, Alison, 'The young at heart", *Guardian*, 18 August 2004.

17 Sieghart, Mary Ann, 'When the tough talk is over, let's listen to sense on crime', *The Times*, 2 December 2004.

18 'More Than 5.6 Million U.S. Residents Have Served Or Are Serving Time In State Or Federal Prisons', US Department of Justice Press Release, 17 August 2003.

19 Glaister, Dan, 'Buried alive under California's law of "three strikes and you're out": Protest marks 10 years of rule that means decades in jail for minor theft', *Guardian*, 8 March 2004.

J.C. Lester

1 New York: Broadway Books, 1997.

2 The two rightly celebrated introductions to this ideology are Friedman, D.D., *The Machinery of Freedom: Guide to Radical Capitalism*, (1973) 2nd edn, La Salle, Ill: Open Court, 1989; and Rothbard, M.N., *For a New Liberty: The Libertarian Manifesto*, (1973) rev. edn, New York: Macmillan Co., 1978.

3 For a more detailed and philosophical exposition of the position taken here see Lester, J.C., 'Libertarian Rectification: restitution, retribution, and the risk-multiplier', *Journal of Value Inquiry* 34, no. 2-3 (2000): 287-297, or Lester, J.C., *Escape From Leviathan: Liberty, Welfare and Anarchy Reconciled*, Basingstoke: Macmillan, New York: St Martin's Press, 2000, pp. 108-120.

4 F. A. Hayek has famously distinguished spontaneously evolved law from state legislation in his *Law, Legislation and Liberty*, London: Routledge & Kegan Paul, (1973-79), 1982. But as a classical liberal, rather than a libertarian, he thinks that state legislation can be a useful supplement. See also Leoni, B., *Freedom and the Law*, (1961) expanded 3rd edn, Indianapolis: Liberty Fund, 1991.

5 All victims of this type of crime have a claim of this sort, but if more than one in ten aggressors starts being caught then the risk-multiplier eventually comes down in proportion.

6 I suspect there are difficulties with my current formulation of the risk-multiplier but my intuition is that some consistent version of it is possible and correct.

7 During the course of a crime, the risk-multiplier restitution that would be owed if the aggressor escapes means the victim can retaliate up to that value. It will be very approximate at the time, of course, but it means that the victim has clear leeway to be more violent than the criminal (even, in restitutive retribution, as the criminal is fleeing: this might

be seen as a more just version of the 'Outlaw' view that
Murray defends).

8   Here I agree with Bruce L. Benson, and disagree with some
other libertarians, that there is room in libertarian
restitution for retribution (i.e., that restitution may be taken
in the form of retribution). See Benson, B.L., 'Restitution in
Theory and Practice', *Journal of Libertarian Studies* 12, no. 1
(1996): 75–97.

9   For instance, see Benson, B.L., *The Enterprise of Law: Justice
without the State*, San Francisco: Pacific Research Institute
for Public Policy, 1990.